T0319847

Structured products

With the advent of structured products, institutional investors are required both to have a strong technical knowledge, yet also the flair to move swiftly on their instincts. This book explains the nature of the principal products. By means of a brief chapter on the basic principles and fundamental rules, this book analyses twenty distinct structures within fixed income and variable income.

This book explains in a practical manner for institutional investors the main structured products that have been developed over the past decade. This is achieved by studying in detail the risks, valuation and key elements of each structured product in turn. The basic principles and underlying philosophy behind the concept are explained in order to give investors a thorough understanding of each product.

The book features details on the following:

● Basic aspects of structured products
● Fundamental aspects used to carry out instrument assessment and risk measurement
● Equity indexed structures
● Fixed income structures
● Ten golden rules of structured products.

ROBERTO KNOP is deputy manager of market risk at Banco Santander Central Hispano where he is responsible for the methodology and quantitative team. He has over ten years experience of derivatives pricing, market risk measurement and also has considerable experience of training others in derivatives pricing and market risk.

STRUCTURED PRODUCTS

STRUCTURED PRODUCTS

A Complete Toolkit to Face Changing Financial Markets

Roberto Knop

JOHN WILEY & SONS, LTD

Other Wiley Editorial Offices

John Wiley & Sons, Inc., 605 Third Avenue,
New York, NY 10158-0012, USA

Wiley-VCH Verlag GmbH, Pappelallee 3,
D-69469 Weinheim, Germany

John Wiley & Sons Australia, Ltd, 33 Park Road, Milton,
Queensland 4064, Australia

John Wiley & Sons (Asia) Pte Ltd, 2 Clementi Loop #02-01,
Jin Xing Distripark, Singapore 129809

John Wiley & Sons (Canada) Ltd, 22 Worcester Road,
Rexdale, Ontario M9W 1L1, Canada

Library of Congress Cataloging-in-Publication Data

A Library of Congress record has been applied for

British Library Cataloguing in Publication Data

A catalogue record for this book is available from the British Library

ISBN 0-471-48647-7

DEDICATION

To Sonia, a wife who is without equal, and whose direct involvement in this work has been fundamental to its success. Also to my son, Roberto, whose birth coincided with the first pages of this book and who reached five months with the last pages.

I offer my thanks and dedication to my parents Roberto and Beatriz for bringing me into this world and for making me the person I am now, and also to my sister Valeria.

Very special thanks also to my grandmother Carmen and in memory of those who are no longer with us. And, of course, I offer my affectionate and sincere dedication to my wife's entire family.

CONTENTS

Foreword   *ix*

General introduction   1

PART I BASIC ASPECTS OF STRUCTURED PRODUCTS   7

  1 Structured products   9
  2 Instrument valuation and risk measurement   13

PART II EQUITY STRUCTURES   31

  3 Warrants   33
  4 Equity deposit   41
  5 Asian deposit   47
  6 Straddle with knockout deposit   55
  7 Digital ranges   63
  8 Reverse convertible   71
  9 Ladder bond   77
10 Basket bond   83
11 Spread bond   91
12 Best-of bond   99

PART III FIXED INCOME STRUCTURES   107

13 Floating rate note   109
14 Reverse floating rate note   115
15 Collared floating rate note   121
16 Digital ranges (corridor notes)   127
17 Step-up callable   133
18 Reset note   139
19 Participating swap   147
20 Performance swap   153

21 Step-up triggered cap   161
22 Constant maturity bond   171

Appendix A Ten golden rules   *179*
Appendix B Characteristics from the buyer's viewpoint   *181*

Bibliography   *183*

Index

FOREWORD

The rapid change that has come about in international financial markets over recent years has led to a transformation in the way risks are managed. Risk management has had to be redefined to cope with innovative and sophisticated approaches to investment. In the euro-zone, the main financial bodies have had to match their approach to the new environment, and they have had to become more competitive to face the challenges of banking in the twenty-first century. The spread of globalisation, boosted by a breathtaking advance in technology, is encouraging greater specialisation in financial banking services. This allows the client to enjoy a greater range of products for specific needs, accompanied by a renewed thrust in wholesale banking, from management itself to the control and measurement of new risks in the financial markets.

The Santander Central Hispano Group has shown it is sensitive to these changes and has adapted to the needs of the client in a strongly competitive environment. Santander Central Hispano has exemplified this new approach which the markets now demand from business chiefs. It has expanded nationally and internationally, especially within the euro-zone and Latin America. And it is still expanding, by giving the greater guarantees required and by adapting to the specific needs of the economies, clients and markets. Structured products, or high added value products, have been developed by the bank as a business tool and they will continue to be developed, especially in the new emerging markets. The competitive edge that Santander Central Hispano is believed to possess, given its knowledge of the instruments and its knowledge of the markets, makes structured products a mainstay of the group's wholesale banking activities. But it all depends on the ability to measure and control the inherent risks, and Santander Central Hispano has accorded this top priority.

Written by one of our professionals, this financial manual succinctly describes the characteristics, the risks, the construction and the valuation for each of the main structured products. Within the financial markets there appears to be an unmistakable trend towards structured products. They are seeking to adapt to the specific needs of the client. And readers will find clear answers to many questions that arise, both from the investor's viewpoint and from the issuer's. To measure the risk in a structured product, it's necessary to know how it was constructed. All these aspects are tackled here in considerable detail; they profit from the author's meticulous attention to detail and they are matched by a clarity drawn from his experience.

Finally, Santander Central Hispano and its team of professionals demonstrate once more their ability to meet the needs of the client, and on this occasion, to sponsor a work which will, I consider, make a significant contribution to the financial and academic world.

Matias Rodríguez Inciarte
Vice-Chairman
Banco Santander Central Hispano

GENERAL INTRODUCTION

The development and growth in financial markets during the 1980s marked a change in quality, a change of historical significance. During that relatively short period, investors increased their risk diversification strategies and became more sophisticated in their management approach, within a more competitive context. The investment bank has constantly had to move towards new financial instruments capable of satisfying the increasingly specialised needs of investors and those taking risks. The growing flow of funds has been subjected to economic swings, on an international scale, in ways which have become more and more varied among industrialised and emerging economies. They are calling for new ways to be protected. And faced with the growing needs of obtaining finance, emerging economies have also had to bring in new strategies to acquire resources. In short, a set of natural market forces determined that, during the 1980s and 1990s, a very special activity within the management of capital would arise or intensify, an activity called structuring. The professionals involved were not just economists; they included physicists, engineers and mathematicians, and they have given us a whole new approach to investment.

These structuring professionals demonstrate several special qualities: an extraordinary imagination, a high technical qualification in pure science, and a capacity for construction and design, particularly in other disciplines. Any finance institution that takes positions in structured products has to deal within a competitive environment in traditional finance, within a banking system which has become more and more professional in its approach. Without doubt, that greater professional approach within banking is the result of the greater professional approach of their investors, even among the smallest. Nowadays the business of structuring is not an exhausted issue in many economies, not even in so-called industrialised economies. This is because business depends on the limitless capacity of human imagination and the specific needs of the investor.

This book endeavours to give an absolutely practical approach to the main structured products appearing in financial markets over the past ten years. And it tries to answer questions which may arise in investment dealings. On many occasions, these questions have been raised unwittingly, as the *structurer* seeks to achieve a maximisation in profits. Part 1 introduces the basic principles and fundamental rules of the game, and these are used to analyse twenty distinct products within interest rate and equity linked income. Four aspects are examined for each structure:

- Definition and commercial presentation
- Risks
- Construction
- Valuation

I have had professional experience in two distinct fields: as an investment analyst and consultant, and as a risk analyst for a large bank. These risks were taken on by business concerns as they sent out structured products. This experience, from two perspectives, has allowed me to form a slightly clearer picture of the advantages, disadvantages and risks contained in these instruments.

First we must try to find out what exactly is a structured product. In the full certainty that alternative definitions may prove valid, we can say that a structured product is a financial instrument and its return depends on the composition of other, simpler products. A structured product usually consists of a loan, in its various forms, and one or more derivative products. The special feature here will be the conversion of the original risks of each of its components. The aim is to generate added value, as much for assets as liabilities, and be adaptable in the way most appropriate to the specific needs, expectations and profiles of the risks. This is all viable if we can achieve higher operational margins or profit levels adjusted to the risk.

Another essential task is to define and identify the main players. For this purpose we will talk about *investors* and *issuers*. In essence, these two figures can amount to the central axis points. However, as may be confirmed on many occasions, the 'initial' issuer for any structure will have been the 'excuse' for this, with the figure of the *structurer* emerging and gaining prominence. In these cases the convertible action of the original risks, by means of this agent, is so great that in practice the final product which reaches the investor bears only a slight resemblance to the original product launched by the issuer. Then the added value of the structurer will be translated into greater financial rewards, which will probably fall on the shoulders of the investor. In these cases it is not in vain that the original issuer may end up assuming some risks, which are very distinct from those assumed by the investor, not only in sign but also in form. In other cases, where the structurer restricts himself to 'wholesaling' the structured products, there will be almost total symmetry of the risks between investor and issuer, in terms of form but not sign.

Here are the main advantages for investors:

- Diversifying the assets
- Diversifying and filtering the risks
- Measured investment
- Flexibility
- Gearing
- Access to over-the-counter (OTC) markets

Here are the main disadvantages for investors:

- More restricted secondary markets
- Greater risks or risks that are less evident in certain products

Here are the main advantages for issuers:

- Lower financial cost
- Gearing
- More perfect hedging

Here are the main disadvantages for investors:

- Greater difficulty in measuring risk
- They are not pure derivatives (they are not outside the balance sheet)
- They have to manage more dynamic forms of hedging

Traditionally there have been three distinguishable classifications:

- According to the 'generation' component in relation to degree of complexity of the distinct parts of the structure (today up to three generations are distinguished clearly)
- According to commitment to the principal (guaranteed or non-guaranteed convertibles)
- According to the financial nature of the structures

This book uses the last classification – financial nature – and draws a clear distinction between financial structures of fixed income and equity income.

Fully compatible with these classifications is the analysis of structured products according to whether they are *assets* or *liabilities*. In products relating to *assets*, a greater profitability is pursued with limitation of assumed risk. In products referring to liabilities, the reductions in cost-related risk to market risk constitute its *raison d'être*.

Although we are dealing here with questions that are initially semantic in nature, the title given to the structures will sometimes have implications on regulations and treatment, especially those issued with the task of raising liabilities. In this sense, many regulatory bodies insist that grading of deposits as a sole right is permitted only to those structures which guarantee the principal, and they leave the title 'bonds' for those which do not do this. In our later analysis we will not be confined to the title of any structure by virtue of the type of guarantee offered about the principal.

For each of the structures we will analyse, we will be dealing with the basic inherent risks; nevertheless, it will normally be of special interest to look at how the issuer of a structure will succeed in managing the original risk that was created during the operation. In fact, as we will be able to observe, the issuer of a structure will have two basic ways to deal with this:

- Assume the natural risk, which is obviously consistent with a view of the financial variables involved in the structure, contrary to that of the investor. This would show that in this case the activity of creating the structure answers a need determined in relation to desired growth of the variables, more than a business activity in itself.
- Assume hedging of the original risks in such a way that the value of risk obtained by the primary structure would be higher than the costs generated by the hedge. By right, the said margin being shown is a banking activity focused on the generation of value in itself, by means of the structure provided to the final customer. This is the most usual way in investment banking.

Within the second approach, three types of risk must be managed:

- Market
- Liquidity
- Credit

For the investor, structuring will basically convert and translate the original risks of its components, when it makes its map of investors fit into a spectrum more in tune with its special vision. The reason why the final investor seldom opts for this conversion answers the question of economies of scale and efficient use of comparative advantages, which derivative products allow, even the simplest ones.

Besides that, the generation of wholesale products presupposes an additional source of relative price reduction for the small investor. This must be dealt with promptly when evaluating a structured product. Even though it is possible to overcome the well-prepared technical answer, especially once you have read this book, limitations on price competitiveness, which can be obtained to generate structures on a small scale, will be a determining factor in the final valuation. It is not without reason that people ask: Why are we here today buying a car instead of building it ourselves? Or perhaps more realistically, why do we buy bread instead of making it? It is of course a question of money, necessary means, or time, which ultimately amount to the same thing.

PART I

BASIC ASPECTS OF STRUCTURED PRODUCTS

1

STRUCTURED PRODUCTS

When should you invest in a structured product?

Investment in a structured product must always be carried out in answer to the two basic questions:

- Can the structure adapt itself to the expectations we have of the implied market variables?
- Is the price we are being asked approximately the price that would be obtained in conditions of financial equilibrium, and does it replicate each of the structure's parts?

The two questions, or rather their answers, are of equal relevance. An affirmative answer to both is the necessary condition and is sufficient to tackle the investment. To give them a real-life context, imagine you are reading some publicity for a new model of car. The two basic questions then become: Do I need the car? And, relatively speaking, is their asking price suitable and competitive?

The investor must keep clearly in mind the answers to these questions. A no to the first question – the structure does not fit its special vision of the market – can lead to a direct rejection. But the answer to the second question might be so positive that the investor may then think about speculating or arbitraging in his purchase. That's to say, he might in theory purchase something so cheaply (at the margin of what matches our expectations) that he then sells it immediately afterwards at a higher price, according to market conditions. A negative answer to the second question must lead the investor to reject the investment, or at least to consider his answer along alternative lines. The following analyses investigate these ideas but without falling into pure theory.

The analysis would be incomplete without considering tax issues. Although taxation is not a central topic of this book, issuers and investors must pay special attention to the regulations applicable to structured products when they evaluate potential profits and costs. In many European countries it is not unusual to have several structured products issued for more than two years just because of the tax advantages for the investors. Depending on the regulations in force, the real profitability of an investment in a structured product can differ considerably from country to country.

How are risks measured in structured products?

Investor and issuer both face new risks within structured products. Despite signs to the contrary, the risk assumed by the issuer of a structure is not always the same as the risk assumed by the investor. It is a fact that the structurer's paper will be the determining factor in this sense. The case is very clear when, for example, a company sends out a bond with a special structure which reaches the investor without any conversions. This is as opposed to the case in which the same bond is converted by the structurer (bank) into some of its characteristics or risks, with more aggressive commercial targets, or aimed at fixed targets.

Many of these situations are seen in more straightforward structures such as *floating rate notes* and *constant maturity treasuries*. In these cases, thanks to the structurer's role, the real financing terms taken on by the issuer may be contrary to the investment terms, which are tackled by the funds dealer. A situation may arise where an issuer pays fixed interest rates at the same time as the investor receives floating interest rates. In these cases, who initially assumes the conversion risk which has occurred on the way? It is the structurer. In fact, he will cash this in, rather than assume this risk, and he will do this to take on its management and hedging.

Is there any sense in covering a purchased structure?

To do this at the point of acquisition would be tantamount to borrowing money to lend it, but without the perspective of getting any profits from that intermediation. There may be more than a little sense in considering hedging for a structure acquired previously which has since generated certain profits or has accumulated losses.

In these cases, what will become practically inevitable are some costs to cover this. In a structure's case, where there is a desire to consolidate the profit which has accumulated up to date, it is to be hoped that the cover allowed by this objective reduces the income obtained in relative terms. This hedge involves the adoption of positions contrary to each of the instruments comprising the primary structured operation. That is why the fundamental point is to know the form and content of a structure. It is then possible to close or cover it perfectly at market price. Nor should it be said that, where there is a wish to close a structure which has generated losses up to the present, that it will also involve a cost which must be added to the accumulated income. Also, the instruments involved in this will mean the adoption of individual positioning (by product), contrary to those defined in the primary structure. On many occasions, however, given the exotic character of the structure's components and the liquidity these instruments may hold in the markets, perfect hedging is hard to obtain. Each analysis will look at these questions in detail.

It is also relevant to consider the interest rate curves that are used in making valuations. A large part of analysing complex financial structures is based on updating future cash flow movements. Even though these may be combined with derivative products, conceptual errors in updating cash flow movements will be the deciding factors when final valuations are made.

When we talk about interest rate curves, we must carry out a basic classification that includes the credit rating of the issuer of the financial movements we are analysing. If we simplify as much as possible the world in which we will be working, then we should be able to say there will be at least three categories:

- The very highest risk
- Interbank risk
- Risk in dealings with corporations and companies having different ratings

But this classification may have opponents, since there does not appear to be any clarification within the interbank context. Certainly, from an orthodox viewpoint, it would be necessary to apply distinct interbank curves according to the financial institution being considered, yet in many markets this practice is still not usual. In operating investment and financing through interbank deposits, or in quoting for implied volatility options, for short-term rates or variable income, it is difficult to detect segmentation according to credit rating. However, variations may be seen in volume and time in spreads of purchase or sale at time of quoting.

What are the two fundamental structuring schemes when raising funds?

Guaranteed products

Guaranteed products enable a liability to be gained which guarantees the principal for the investor, so that apart from the raising itself, it may be invested in zero coupon deposits. This leaves the rest for acquisition of derivatives, which will be sent to the investor, and for the corresponding earnings.

Investment in risk-free zero coupon deposits is the minimum necessary to guarantee the investor 100% return, or part of the principal invested, until maturity of the structure. The investor in guaranteed products will definitely receive a derivative and knows in advance what percentage of the principal he will obtain, in whatever case, until the maturity date. The only thing remaining is to determine the final interest rate level.

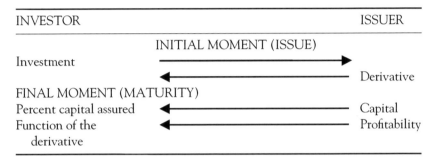

Non-guaranteed products

Non-guaranteed products, or reverse convertibles, are where the investor irrevocably takes on asset acquisition at a determined price (the issuer's put) at the point when he implicitly takes on a zero coupon deposit with maturity equal to the structure negotiated. The attractive thing about these structures is usually in the relatively higher coupons offered. Radical changes in the development of the market will involve complications in how the issuer manages this. The investor will definitely surrender a derivative within the reverse convertible, and in exchange he is offered a potentially greater profit level to other forms of investment. It is not known beforehand what percentage of the principal invested will be obtained on the maturity date. It only remains now to determine the final profit level. There is no way of knowing the payback percentage. But this is compensated by a potentially higher profit level offered on the product.

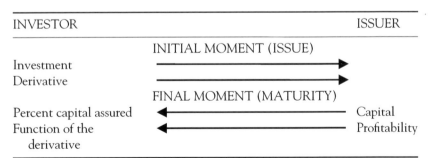

2

INSTRUMENT VALUATION AND RISK MEASUREMENT

Basic concepts associated with interest rates

We will need to perform cash flow valuations and capitalisations, and for this we will need fixed interest rate instalments. Starting with these, it will be possible to calculate corresponding discount factors, or to obtain present values in a future monetary unit. Different instruments will require different techniques for calculating the discount factors.

If we use interbank deposit interest rates, we can immediately calculate the corresponding discount factors. Currency conventions must be considered when *spot* or cash operations are discussed. Here are the possibilities:

- *Spot* = 0 *days*: the operation is carried out at spot value on the same day as the agreement is made
- *Spot* = 1 *day*: the operation is carried out at spot value on the next working day following the agreement
- *Spot* ≥ 2 *days*: the operation is carried out at spot value on an unspecified working day that comes two or more days after the agreement is made

Here are the discount factors for the spot date in each case:

$$DF_{spot} = 1 \text{ for spot} = 0 \text{ days}$$

$$DF_{spot} = DF_{overnight} \text{ for spot = 1 day}$$

$$DF_{spot} = DF_{tom \, next} \text{ for spot} \geq 2 \text{ days}$$

Discount factors for overnight (1 day starting from spot) and tom next (from day after tomorrow) are calculated in a similar way:

$$DF_{overnight} = \frac{1}{1 + r_{ON} YF_{ON}} \qquad (2.1)$$

$$FD_{tom \, next} = \frac{FD_{overnight}}{1 + r_{TN} YF_{TN}} \qquad (2.2)$$

where

DF = discount factor
r = market interest rate
ON = overnight
TN = tom next
YF = fraction of year, which we will calculate up to the year as
     $YF_i = n/basis$
n = number of interest accrual days according to convention
     (usually in real days)
basis = number of days in a year which, according to the currency under
     discussion, will vary between 360 or 365/366 days

Here are the most usual ways for reckoning fractions of a year:

$$\text{Actual}/360 = \frac{D_2 - D_1}{360} \qquad (2.3)$$

$$\text{Actual}/365 = \frac{D_2 - D_1}{365} \qquad (2.4)$$

$$30/360 = \frac{\Delta_{30}(D_2, D_1)}{360} \qquad (2.5)$$

$$\text{Act}/\text{Act} = \frac{D_2 - D_1}{D_i - D_{i-1_{year}}} \qquad (2.6)$$

where

D_1 = initial date
D_2 = final date
D_i = reference date for the financial event (coupon payment,
             interests, etc.) of the year of the valuation day (i)

$\Delta_{30}(D_2 - D_1) =$ the difference in days between two dates assuming 30 days per month and is calculated using
$$\Delta_{30}(D_2, D_1) = [360(y_2 - y_1) + 30(m_2 - m_1) + (d_2 - d_1)]$$
with $y =$ years, $m =$ months, $d =$ days

If we start with equation (2.1), we obtain interbank deposit rate discount factors (usually up to one year's term):

$$DF_i = \frac{DF_{spot}}{1 + r_i YF_i} \qquad (2.7)$$

For terms greater than one year, where no quotations exist for interbank deposits, another instrument must be used which has the same type of generic creditworthy risk. The more usual alternatives are interest rate futures or interest rates swaps (IRS).

An IRS is a derivative product for which the buyer acquires the payment obligation over a period of time and at an agreed fixed interest rate over a determined frequency of payments. This takes place during operation of the principal, which alone serves as reference and cannot be exchanged. In return for this, the buyer will receive from the IRS seller a floating interest rate linked to a money market index over a period of time and at an agreed frequency of payments.

This takes place during the operation of the principal, which alone serves as reference and cannot be exchanged. At the point of agreement, the current value of all cash flows of the IRS fixed branch is exactly the same as the value corresponding to the estimated variable, starting from implicit rates. Consequently, the value of the IRS sold will be the difference between the current value of the future flows of the fixed branch and the current value of the future flows of the floating branch, which have been estimated from the implicit rates' starting point. At the moment of reaching an IRS market agreement, this difference is equal to zero.

$$\sum_{i=1}^{n}(r_{fixed})_i YF_i \times DF_i \times notional - \sum_{i=1}^{m}(r_{implicit})_i YF_i \times DF_i \times notional \quad (2.8)$$

where

notional $=$ notional amount
r_{fixed} $=$ fixed interest rate
YF $=$ fraction of year in which it accrues
DF $=$ discount factor
n $=$ number of fixed flows

m = number of floating flows
r_{implicit} = implicit interest rate

Given the two implicit deposit interest rates i_a, i_b, we obtain

$$r_{\text{implicit}} = \left(\frac{1 + r_b d_b / 36\,000}{1 + r_a d_a / 36\,000} - 1 \right) \frac{36\,000}{d_b - d_a} \tag{2.9}$$

where

r_a = interest rate of deposit a (shortest period of those implied)
r_b = interest rate of deposit b (longest period of those implied)
d_a = days of life of deposit a (shortest period of those implied)
d_b = days of life of deposit b (longest period of those implied)

The interest payment frequency of one branch and the interest payment frequency of another branch do not usually coincide. Even though the IRS are derivatives obtained over the counter (OTC), or non-standardised, e.g. IRS nominated in euros, and through market conventions, floating interests are paid at a six-monthly rate, as opposed to fixed interests which are paid annually.

Suppose a three-year IRS quotes a rate of 5%; this means that the buyer of the IRS is bound legally to pay annually, over the life of the IRS, a 5% interest rate at the end of each period. This is in exchange for receiving the six-month Euribor rate every six months, according to the conditions defined by this index in each commencement period.

When we consider that, in the market, quoted IRS rates correspond to interests payable at a determined rate, not as one payment (as for interbank deposits), then calculation of the corresponding discount factors requires a special technique. This technique is called *bootstrapping* and relies not only on the IRS rates but also on the interbank market rates. This in fact is how the mechanism is started. So once the discount factors are known, up to one year after the interbank deposits start, according to equation (2.7) and given the IRS rates (which are not zero coupon rates), then any discount factor higher than one year will be given as

$$DF_i = \frac{DF_{\text{spot}} - IRS_i \sum_{j=1}^{i-1} DF_j YF_j}{1 + (IRS_i YF_i)} \tag{2.10}$$

where IRS is the market IRS rate for the term. Notice how this is an iterative mechanism; the discount factors of terms $n - i$ have to be calculated by starting from a one-year discount factor. Let's look at an example. Given the following information, let's calculate the discount factor to three years.

- Spot discount factor: 0.999777
- One-year deposit rate: 5% (suppose 365 days on the basis of Act/360)
- Two-year IRS rate: 5.25% (suppose 722 days on the basis of 30/360)
- Three-year IRS rate: 5.50% (suppose 1084 days on the basis of 30/360)

$$DF_{1 \ year} = \frac{0.999777}{1 + (5\% \times 365/360)} = 0.951540$$

$$DF_{2 \ year} = \frac{0.999777 - 5.25\%(0.951540 \times 360/360)}{1 + (5.25\% \times 362/360)} = 0.9021999$$

$$DF_{3 \ year} = \frac{0.999777 - 5.50\%[(0.951540 \times 360/360) + (0.9021999 \times 362/360)]}{1 + (5.50\% \times 362/360)} = 0.850877$$

To calculate the term discount factors, which do not correspond to market rate standards, interpolations should be applied. For interest rates, it is admissible to employ linear interpolations and this is what usually happens:

$$i_i = \frac{i_a(d_b - d_i) + i_b(d_i - d_a)}{d_b - d_a} \tag{2.11}$$

where

i_i = interest rate to be interpolated
i_a = previous interest rate
i_b = subsequent interest rate
d_i = number of days for interpolated rate
d_a = number of days for previous rate
d_b = number of days for subsequent rate

Starting with these interpolated rates, the corresponding discount factors, $DF_{1 \ year}$ to $DF_{3 \ year}$, should be obtained. Alternatively, in the case of interpolating within discount factors, instead of doing this on interest rates, it is recommended to apply exponential interpolations:

$$DF_i = DF_a \left(\frac{DF_a}{DF_b}\right)^{(d_i - d_a)/(d_b - d_a)} \tag{2.12}$$

Treatment of fixed income asset risk

The value of fixed income assets, and specifically periodic coupon bonds, is given by the sum of the present value of their cash flows, under a supposed simplifier in the rate or interest rate being evaluated. Use of the yield to

maturity as the only rate to carry out evaluation of all cash flows, together
with the zero coupon rate, is general practice in valuation of periodic coupon
bonds.

$$\text{Price} = \sum_{i=1}^{n} \frac{F_i}{(1 + \text{YTM})^{\text{YF}_i}}$$

where

F = cash flows
TM = yield to maturity
YF = year fraction

There are several basic measures of YTM price elasticity for standard fixed
income bonds with constant coupons: absolute sensitivity, duration and
modified duration.

Absolute sensitivity (SA)

Price variation in absolute terms with respect to absolute variations of 1% in
the YTM, i.e.

$$P_1 - P_0 \approx -\text{SA}(\text{YTM}_1 - \text{YTM}_0) \tag{2.13}$$

Absolute sensitivity is the first derivative of the function, where price is related
to the YTM:

$$\text{Sensitivity} = \sum_{i=1}^{n} \frac{F_i(\text{YF}_i)}{(1 + \text{YTM})^{\text{YF}_i+1}} \tag{2.14}$$

Modified duration (MD)

Price variation in percentage terms with respect to absolute variations of 1%
in the YTM, i.e.

$$\frac{P_1 - P_0}{P_0} \approx -\text{MD}(\text{YTM}_1 - \text{YTM}_0) \tag{2.15}$$

By adapting the equation of absolute sensitivity to a relative variation in price,
we obtain

$$\text{Modified duration} = \frac{1}{P} \sum_{i=1}^{n} \frac{F_i(\text{YF}_i)}{(1 + \text{YTM})^{\text{YF}_i+1}} \tag{2.16}$$

Macaulay duration (D)

Price variation in percentage terms with respect to percentage variations of 1% in the YTM, i.e.

$$\frac{P_1 - P_0}{P_0} \approx -D\frac{YTM_1 - YTM_0}{YTM_0} \qquad (2.17)$$

By adapting the equation of modified duration to a relative variation, also in YTM, we obtain

$$\text{Duration} = \frac{1}{P}\sum_{i=1}^{n}\frac{F_i(YF_i)}{(1 + YTM)^{YF_i}} \qquad (2.18)$$

This allows the duration to be defined as the average residual life of the title's cash flows, weighted by the present value in these.

Basic concepts associated with financial options

In many of the structures we will analyse, various kinds of option will be present. Let's remember that, for the person who acquires it, an option is a right to buy or sell an asset, on a future date or during a period of time, at a fixed price, called the strike price. A premium will be paid for that right. The types of right acquired may be divided into purchase, or call, and sale, or put.

A call grants the right to buy an underlying asset (asset for which the option is nominated), on a future date or during a period of time up to a future date, at a pre-established strike. A premium must be paid to the seller or issuer of the option for this right. The option seller is obliged to sell the asset at strike price if the option buyer decides to exercise this right. Naturally, the option buyer will exercise his right when the underlying asset's market price at the moment of decision is above the option's strike price. A net profit would then materialise if the difference obtained between market price and strike price were higher than the premium paid.

A put is the right to sell an underlying asset, on a future date or during a period of time up to a future date, at a pre-established strike. A premium must be paid to the seller or issuer of the option for this right. The option seller is obliged to buy the asset at strike price if the option buyer elects to exercise this right, which is to sell. Naturally, the option buyer will exercise his right, when the underlying asset's market price at the moment of decision is lower than the option's strike price. A positive result would then materialise if the difference obtained between strike price and market price were higher than the premium paid.

The most standard type of option is the European option. Its only possible strike is when the option matures. Another type is the American option, where the strike is possible at any moment during the option's life until it matures or expires. Later on we will be looking at more exotic types of option, where their definition breaks away from these standard types. But by identifying a few basic risk parameters, we can obtain a clearer understanding of the profitability and risk profiles for structures incorporating any type of optional component.

The value of a European call or put, where strike is only possible on maturity, is a function of several items:

- *Price of the underlying asset*: the asset's market price for which the option is nominated
- *Strike price of the option*: purchase price (call) or sale price (put) agreed on the option
- *Implied volatility*: volatility quoted in the market and which the market assigns to the future movement in underlying asset price for the life of the option
- *Risk-free interest rate*: market interest rate corresponding to the existing term between date of valuation and maturity of the option
- *Dividends paid by the underlying asset*: dividends accrued by the asset for which the option is nominated during the option's life
- *Time to maturity of the option*: fraction of year between the date of valuation and the date of maturity

The Black–Scholes model is a major model for options valuation and it can be applied to European options. Here are its main assumptions:

- The markets function without transaction costs or taxes; the values negotiated are infinitely divisible and can be operated continuously
- The risk-free interest rate is known and constant throughout the time
- The investors may lend and owe at the risk-free interest rate
- There is no limit to the level of overdrawn sale
- The underlying asset price follows a Wiener process with constant variance

For asset options which pay dividends, we have the following equations:

$$\text{Call} = e^{-qT}SN(d_1) - Ke^{-rT}N(d_2) \tag{2.19}$$

$$\text{Put} = -e^{-qT}SN(-d_1) + Ke^{-rT}N(-d_2) \tag{2.20}$$

$$d_1 = \frac{\ln(S/K) + (r - q + \frac{1}{2}\sigma^2)T}{\sigma\sqrt{T}}$$

$$d_2 = d_1 - \sigma\sqrt{T}$$

$$q = -(1/T)\ln[1 - \text{NPV(dividends)}/S]$$

where

S = underlying asset price
K = strike
σ = volatility
r = risk-free interest rate
q = continuous dividend yield
T = time to option maturity in years

and NPV(dividends) is the net present value of future dividend payments. Using these equations, we can obtain the option's sensitivities to distinct, relevant variables. In fact, there are five quantities we can obtain analytically.

Delta

Delta represents variations in the option's value for unit variations in the underlying asset price:

$$\text{Delta for call} = e^{-qT}N(d_1) \tag{2.21}$$

$$\text{Delta for put} = e^{-qT}(N(d_1) - 1) \tag{2.22}$$

Gamma

Gamma represents variations in delta for unit variations in the underlying asset; gamma measures the sensitivity of delta:

$$\frac{1}{S\sigma\sqrt{T}}\left[\frac{1}{\sqrt{2\pi}}\exp\left(\frac{-d_1^2}{2}\right)\right]\exp(-qT) \tag{2.23}$$

Vega

Vega represents the variations in the option's value for variations of 1% in the implied volatility:

$$\frac{S\sqrt{T}}{100}\left[\frac{1}{\sqrt{2\pi}}\exp\left(\frac{-d_1^2}{2}\right)\right]\exp(-qT) \tag{2.24}$$

Theta

Theta represents variation in the value of a call over one day as an outcome of the remaining constant variables:

$$-\frac{Se^{-qT}N(d_1)\sigma}{2\sqrt{T}} + qSN(d_1)e^{-qT} - rKe^{-rT}N(d_2) \tag{2.25}$$

And for a put:

$$-\frac{Se^{-qT}N(d_1)\sigma}{2\sqrt{T}} - qSN(-d_1)e^{-qT} + rKe^{-rT}N(-d_2) \qquad (2.26)$$

Rho

Rho represents the variations in a call's value as a result of 1% variations in interest rate to maturity of the option:

$$TKe^{-rT}N(d_2) \qquad (2.27)$$

And for a put:

$$-TKe^{-rT}N(-d_2) \qquad (2.28)$$

Some general conclusions

The buyer obtains profits from a call (the seller suffers losses):

- Price rises in the underlying asset
- Increase in price volatility of the underlying asset
- Rise in interest rate until the option matures
- Reductions in dividends paid by the underlying asset

The buyer obtains profits from a put (the seller suffers losses):

- Price falls in the underlying asset
- Increase in price volatility of the underlying asset
- Fall in interest rate until option matures
- Reductions in dividends paid by the underlying asset

In general, the risks taken on by the buyer, call or put, are limited to the premium paid by the option, whereas the seller has a 'limitless' risk, through the variables already pointed out. The options buyer suffers from the course of time, in that time removes value from the option until its maturity date. Some of these claims will become clearer when they are examined for specific options later in the book.

Calculating value at risk (VaR): the basics

The value at risk (VaR) is a basic measure of market risk; it aims to quantify the maximum loss which may occur in the value of a portfolio of financial instruments, and is associated with a statistically determined confidence level for a specified holding period. Since the 1990s, people have increasingly recognised the importance of taking into account specific market risk measures. In this way, J. P. Morgan launched a framework to estimate, among other things, the VaR, under the name RiskMetrics Methodology.

At about the same time, the main financial bodies around the world, in cooperation with researchers, tried to push forward in this direction. So today we can clearly identify two large groups working on methods to calculate VaR:

- Methodologies using set parameters are based on variance and covariance in the rates of change of financial asset prices; several assumptions have been made about these rates of variation.
- Methodologies using simulations
  - Historical methods use historical rates of price variation for financial assets; these rates are then used in simulations to generate current and future values.
  - Monte Carlo methods use random number generators to produce rates of price variation for financial assets; these rates are then used in simulations to generate current and future values.

Combinations or modifications of these two large groups are used in financial institutions all around the world. The simulation techniques rely on important backing from academic and technical bodies, especially in dealing with the risk of derivative products. This academic work elucidates the technical detail behind these methodologies and underpins the ideas about structured products described in this book.

Parametric methods

When appropriate, the parametric techniques for calculating VaR prove particularly easy for certain types of asset. The typical case is a portfolio of shares or currencies. The parametric VaR, assuming a fixed type of probability distribution of its returns or variation rates, is given by

$$\text{VaR} = \text{market value} \times \sigma \times \text{NSTD} \times \sqrt{T}$$

where

σ = standard deviation or historical volatility in asset price variations for horizons equal to T
T = holding period in days, for which the VaR requires calculation
NSTD = number of standard deviations for the chosen confidence level and the chosen distribution

The normal distribution function is one of the most commonly used. However, in the treatment of derivatives, it is not always the most suitable. In option derivatives, where there is higher convexity, this technique is not recommended, although its clarity makes it look attractive.

For a portfolio of two distinct assets, the total net VaR is given by

$$\text{VaR} = [\text{VaR}_i^2 + \text{VaR}_j^2 + 2\rho_{ij}\text{VaR}_i\text{VaR}_j]^{1/2}$$

where i and j denote assets i and j, and ρ_{ij} is the correlation between the returns of i and j. Generally this is given by

$$\text{VaR} = \left[\sum_{i=1}^{N} a_i^2\text{VaR}_i^2 + 2 \sum_{i=1}^{N} \sum_{j=1,i\neq j}^{N} a_i a_j \rho_{ij}\text{VaR}_i\text{VaR}_j \right]^{1/2}$$

where a is the asset weight.

Example

Let's suppose we have a portfolio of three shares (A, B, C), in each of which we have invested €1000. With knowledge of the historical information on the volatilities and correlations, we will calculate, parametrically, the daily value at risk, assuming the losses and gains of the portfolio have a normal (Gaussian) distribution with average zero. We will assume 99% confidence (2.326 standard deviations).

- Daily volatility of A = 2.95%
- Daily volatility of B = 6.08%
- Daily volatility of C = 2.03%

The correlation grid is as follows; all figure are percentages.

	Share A	Share B	Share C
Share A	100	50.80	12.43
Share B	50.80	100	6.37
Share C	12.43	6.37	100

$$\text{VaR A} = 1000 \times 2.95\% \times 2.326 \times \sqrt{1 \text{ day}} = 68.61$$

$$\text{VaR B} = 1000 \times 6.08\% \times 2.326 \times \sqrt{1 \text{ day}} = 141.44$$

$$\text{VaR C} = 1000 \times 2.03\% \times 2.326 \times \sqrt{1 \text{ day}} = 47.25$$

Net correlated VaR to one day would be

$$\left[(68.61 \quad 141.44 \quad 47.25) \begin{pmatrix} 1 & 0.5080 & 0.1243 \\ 0.5080 & 1 & 0.0637 \\ 0.1243 & 0.0637 & 1 \end{pmatrix} \begin{pmatrix} 68.61 \\ 141.44 \\ 47.25 \end{pmatrix} \right]^{1/2} = €196.12$$

It requires more effort to calculate VaR using parametric methodologies when there are interest rate risks to include in the analysis. It will depend on the type of financial instrument being used, but there are usually two options. The first is called cash flow mapping, as described in J. P. Morgan's *Methodology of RiskMetrics*. This converts any future cash flow into current value flows situated at certain standard points in time (points of RiskMetrics). Once the volatilities and correlations in the interest rates are known for the existing point, the next step is to use the VaR methodology to calculate the risks. The second option is to use other parametric methods that instead of activating the nominal future vector flows, use the vector of sensitivities of these same flows to interest rate variations; this is no more than a special feature derived from the methodology of RiskMetrics.

However, when considering the nature of any derivatives within a structured product, it is not recommended to calculate their risks using parametric methods. The assumption of a normal distribution for the losses and gains of these derivatives is rarely a good one, and makes parametric methods even more unsuitable for VaR calculations. We will now have a look at simulation techniques to calculate VaR and other financial market risks.

Historical simulation: easy to follow, simple to use

Step 1: Set the parameters

Define the statistical level of confidence for the way in which the calculation will be made: 1% up to just less than 100%; normally it's between 95% and 99.7%. Choose a holding period (the period for which the expected loss requires estimating); normally it's between 1 day and *n* days. Define the temporary historical window for performing the calculations; it is recommended to use observations over a period of 1 or 2 years. For asset price calculations where the asset prices experience 'structural' changes of increasing frequency, it is recommended to use exponential weightings.

Step 2: Obtain the temporary series

Identify and obtain all temporary price series and relevant interest rates used in measuring risks. These correspond to the historical series of financial variables that today would affect the portfolio value under analysis. Each series or relevant risk factor will be called P_{ix} to indicate the *i*th observed price of the *x*th risk factor.

Step 3: Calculate the historical rates of variation of P_{ix}

In each series of n P_{ix}, we will continuously calculate $n - 1$ variation rates:

$$\ln(P_{ix}/P_{(i-1)x}) \tag{2.29}$$

Step 4: Generate the simulated prices

To the current values of P, i.e. P_n, we will apply the $n-1$ variation rates calculated previously. We will then obtain $n-1$ possible simulated price settings, each with P_x:

$$P_x^e = P_{nx} \exp[\ln(P_{ix}/P_{(i-1)x})] \tag{2.30}$$

Step 5: Generate the simulated proprietary values

By taking the simulated prices, P_x^e, and multiplying them by the quantities q_x of the corresponding instruments in the portfolio being analysed, we obtain the possible market values of this portfolio:

$$V_x^e = P_x^e q_x \tag{2.31}$$

Step 6: Calculate the simulated losses and gains

Put simply, by finding the difference between the simulated proprietary value and the real value of the portfolio, we obtain a result that would hold if instead of considering the real portfolio value, we considered each of the $n-1$ possible settings and obtained a vector of simulated losses and gains.

Step 7: Calculate the percentile of the simulated losses and gains vector

By considering the chosen confidence level, the corresponding percentile will be calculated in order to identify the corresponding estimated loss. So, given a confidence level of $x\%$, we will calculate the percentile $(100 - x)\%$ of the simulated losses and gains vector.

Summary

For structured products, VaR calculated in this way will express the maximum probable loss for the chosen confidence level and holding period. This assumes that the rates of price variation in the structure's components exhibit the same distribution function in the past and over the temporary window of estimation.

An example may help to make things clearer. In a structure composed of various financial instruments, the procedure would be very similar, but instead of one financial instrument, there will be n financial instruments (see steps 5 and 6).

Example

Let's suppose we a have a 1 month call with strike $0.85 per euro, given a spot exchange rate of $0.922 per euro, a 1 month implied volatility of 11.30% and interest rates for dollar and euro of 6.575% and 4.4% respectively. The value of the call would be $0.0733 per euro. If the option nominal were €1 000 000, the premium would be $73 299. Let's calculate the historically simulated VaR by following our seven steps.

Step 1

- Holding period: 1 day
- Confidence level: 99%
- Historical window: 140 most recent days

Step 2

The temporary series are the exchange rate in dollars per euro, 1 month implied volatility, the dollar interest rate and the euro interest rate (Table 2.1).

Step 3

Calculate the variation rates. Having 140 observations, we will have 139 rates as well as 139 scenarios.

Step 4

Create the historical rate simulations for the financial variables (Table 2.2); these are the exchange rates, volatilities, interest rates, etc. Apply them to

Table 2.1								
	STEP 2: Option inputs				STEP 3: Logarithm			
Date	$/€	Volatility	Euro rate	Dollar rate	$/€ (%)	Volatility (%)	Euro rate (%)	Dollar rate (%)
03/01/00	1.009	11.800	3.130	5.740				
04/01/00	1.031	13.100	3.120	5.750	2.11	10.45	−0.32	0.17
⋮	⋮	⋮	⋮	⋮	⋮	⋮	⋮	⋮
18/07/00	0.935	10.500	4.375	6.575	0.01	−2.82	0.00	0.00
19/07/00	0.922	11.300	4.400	6.575	−1.48	7.34	0.57	0.00
20/07/00	0.922	11.300	4.400	6.575	0.04	0.00	0.00	0.00

Table 2.2 Step 4: generate the simulated prices.				
Scenario (days)	$/€	Volatility	Euro rate	Dollar rate
1	0.94	12.54	4.39	6.59
⋮	⋮	⋮	⋮	⋮
137	0.92	10.99	4.40	6.58
138	0.91	12.16	4.43	6.58
139	0.92	11.30	4.40	6.58

current values for the relevant financial variables (latest data 0.922, 11.300, 4.400, 6.575).

Step 5

Generate the option values (Table 2.3) by applying the simulated variables for the previous point, compared to the real position (a 1 month call at 0.85 with nominal of $1 000 000).

Table 2.3 Step 5: simulated option values.	
Scenario (days)	Option value ($)
1	92 864
⋮	⋮
137	73 387
138	60 066
139	73 696

Table 2.4 Step 6: simulated losses and gains.	
Scenario (days)	Option value ($)
1	19.565
⋮	⋮
137	87
138	−13.233
139	397

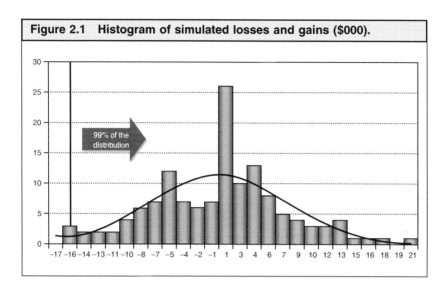

Figure 2.1   Histogram of simulated losses and gains ($000).

Step 6

Knowing that the current option value is $73 299, we can calculate the losses and gains there would be in relation to the possible values found in step 5 (Table 2.4).

Step 7

From the simulated losses and gains vector, we can calculate the percentile 1% (if we take 99% as our confidence level); this gives $16 479, which is the actual VaR being sought (Figure 2.1).

PART II

EQUITY STRUCTURES

3

WARRANTS

Definition and commercial presentation

Warrants give the holder the right to buy (call) or sell (put) a fixed number of underlying asset titles, at a fixed strike price, on a pre-established future date. Under these premises, we might question the qualification of the structured product, once we are talking about an option in its simplest sense. However, given that within a warrant there will exist the portfolio construction work of the funds and the form of titles, we will analyse warrants as structured products.

Commercial practice is very varied, from pure equity warrants to those which produce a combination of assets with equity and fixed income. In its simplest sense, we will find *call warrants* and *put warrants*, through which the investor will obtain a gross profit when the underlying asset market price exceeds the strike price in the first income received.

The strike price is the price at which the buyer of the warrant may buy (call), or sell (put) the underlying asset. Nevertheless, we will see that liquidity does occur, usually through differences, without the need for physical delivery of the underlying. Through these rights, the buyer of the warrant will pay a premium, usually at the moment when the contract is signed. In more standard cases the strike is fixed at the same level as the underlying asset, at the moment when the warrant is agreed. In this way, the buyer of the warrant, if successful, will obtain a derived profit from appreciation or depreciation of the underlying title (according to whether we are dealing with call or put) in terms relative to the real defined price.

There are four major categories of call or put warrants:

- *European warrants*: the right, which they alone incorporate, may be exercised on a fixed date

- *American warrants*: the right, which they incorporate, may be exercised at any moment throughout a period of time until a fixed date
- *Bermudan warrants*: the right, which they incorporate, may be exercised throughout a period of time until a fixed date but on specific dates
- *Asian warrants*: the right, which they incorporate, will not be assessed as far as final title price and strike price are concerned. The buyer of the warrant will take as reference the average between the title price during its operating life and the strike price. This average will be calculated according to a pre-established set of observations within the contract. Other exotic types are also possible

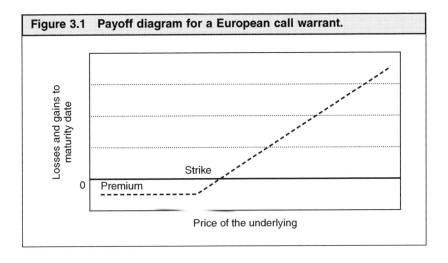

Figure 3.1 Payoff diagram for a European call warrant.

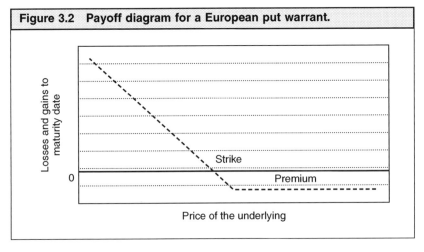

Figure 3.2 Payoff diagram for a European put warrant.

We begin with European warrants:

$$\text{Payoff for a European call warrant} = \max(0, S - K) \qquad (3.1)$$

$$\text{Payoff for a European put warrant} = \max(0, K - S) \qquad (3.2)$$

where

S = underlying price
K = strike

The payoff diagrams are shown in Figures 3.1 and 3.2.

Risks

This structure assumes a basic risk in the price of assets, volatilities, dividends, interest rates and time. When a warrant is purchased, the loss will never be more than the value paid for it (the option premium).

Whoever buys an equity *call warrant* is implicitly demonstrating expectations for some upward price movement in the underlying asset, together with an upward volatility scenario. Besides that, rises in dividends paid out by the asset for which the option is nominated will affect this in a negative way, since the option does not give any right to its call, as long as it does not expire and the title is indeed acquired. Reductions in risk-free market interest rates, and the corresponding risk to the time of option maturity at each moment, will affect the value in a negative way, like the passage of time, if all other variables remain constant.

Whoever buys an equity *put warrant* is implicitly demonstrating some bearish expectations in underlying asset price movement, together with a bullish volatility scenario. Besides that, reductions in dividends paid out by the asset for which the option is nominated will affect this in a negative way. Reductions in risk-free market interest rates, and the corresponding risk to the time of option maturity at each moment, will affect the value in a negative way, like the passage of time, if all other variables remain constant.

In short, we have just described the relationships that exist between the relevant variables and an option's value under the basic hypotheses of standard models such as Black–Scholes. Table 3.1 summarises the relationships

Table 3.1	Sensitivity of share-bearing warrants.								
	Asset price		Volatility		Interest rate		Dividend		Time	
	↑	↓	↑	↓	↑	↓	↑	↓	↑	↓
Call warrant	↑	↓	↑	↓	↑	↓	↓	↑	↑	↓
Put warrant	↓	↑	↑	↓	↓	↑	↑	↓	↑	↓

between the relevant variables and the value of the warrant. Note that maximum risk for the buyer of the warrant is limited to the price paid for it.

Construction

The construction work is slight in relation to its components; a warrant sets up an option call or put for a part or percentage of the underlying asset, in order to give the very best opportunity for gearing. So this determines the warrant's parity – the number of warrants per share. Simply, the unit value of the share option, or title, must be divided by this parity. The most usual units for negotiation are 100, 1000 or 10 000 warrants.

Example

Let's assume we have a one-year BSCH European call warrant worth €0.06 with a strike price of €11 given a current share price of €10. The parity is 10/1 (10 warrants per share). In order to take part in a share at 100% for this parity, there have to be 10 warrants, whose value would be $0.06 \times 10 = €0.60$.

Indicative terms

Description	BSCH €11 call warrant
Unit values	€0.06
Parity	10/1 (10 warrants per share)
Interest	Variable according to BSCH appreciation
Time	1 year
Final payment	Max (BSCH over 1 year) €11

Under the previous conditions, a person investing in 10 warrants knows that, to exercise his rights, the share price should exceed €11. However, taking account of the investment cost, to recover this the price should rise as far as €11.60. Additional rises above this price would generate as great a net profit for the investor as the rise in share price. Note that the final payment is carried out usually through differences between strike price and the instrument price, on the warrant's maturity date, without actual delivery of the asset. In this way, for example, if the BSCH price on the warrant's maturity were at €11.70, the liquidity on behalf of the investor would be

$$11.70 - 11.00 = €0.70$$

The net profit would then be

$$0.70 - 0.60 = €0.10$$

Should the investor really want to hold a BSCH share portfolio on an aforementioned date (10 warrants with parity of 10/1), he would simply consult the market and buy the title at market price, i.e. €11.70, even though its net cost would be €11.60, since he obtained a profit of €0.10 on the option.

Where he does not want to incorporate the actual title in his share portfolio, then the investor should liquidate the warrants, which will generate the corresponding profit obtained with an elevated gearing level, on appreciation of the share. Its cost would only be the premium paid out initially.

Valuation

Valuation of the share options, call or put, within the Black–Scholes model framework is given by the six basic factors in equations (2.19) and (2.20).

Example

Let's look at an example of 10 000 000 European put warrants for the company Telefónica, whose recent growth is shown in Figure 3.3. Here we are dealing with a put with strike €19.60 purchased in March 2000 per €0.095 (parity of 1/1), taking into consideration that the share then was quoted at €30. On that date in August 2000, a month was left before the share reached maturity. Knowing that the current share price is at €21, implied volatility is at 40%,

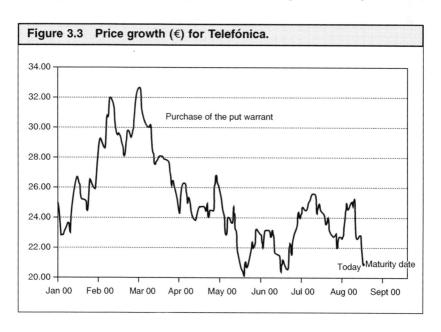

Figure 3.3   Price growth (€) for Telefónica.

risk-free interest rate is at 5%, and assuming the dividend payment is nil, then we will analyse the warrant's situation by evaluating the risks as far as their maturity date. Here is a Black–Scholes valuation for this option:

$$\text{Put} = Ke^{-rT}N(-d_2) - Se^{-qT}N(-d_1)$$
$$= 19.6 \times 2.7812^{-5\% \times 0.082} \times N(-0.5801)$$
$$- 21 \times 2.7182^{-0\% \times 0.082} \times N(-0.6948) = 0.368$$
$$d_1 = \frac{\ln(21/19.6) + [5\% - 0\% + \frac{1}{2}(40\%)^2] \times 0.082}{40\% \times \sqrt{0.082}} = 0.69481$$
$$d_2 = 0.69481 - 40\% \times \sqrt{0.082} = 0.58013$$

In spite of more than five months elapsing, during which the option has lost temporary value, the fall in underlying asset price and the growth in its implied volatility have allowed the option to appreciate in value. To sum up, we would have:

- Value of acquisition: $10\,000\,000 \times 0.095 = €950\,000$
- Current value: $10\,000\,000 \times 0.368 = €3\,680\,000$
- Latent profit: €2 730 000

Strictly speaking, there must be a charge for the cost of financing the investment in this profit, i.e. the €950 000. Moreover, with regards to a European warrant, the gain will not take effect until the maturity date, or until the position is closed, if closure is possible. To close the position, the investor should sell the warrant, which is deemed to be a good purchase, to the original issuer or another interested market agent. This will depend on the market in which it has been acquired, and on the contractual conditions of the original issue.

Where the warrant can be sold to the original issuer, then at market conditions they should pay the €3 680 000. Various reasons might lead the investor to think about closing out this position. The most powerful series would clearly be market expectations, where strike share falls are not foreseen. Bear in mind that, if this were to occur, and where the share finished at say €21, i.e. the current situation, then the put warrant would have nil value on its maturity date, since the strike of €19.60 would not give the person investing (buying) in the warrant any right to a positive strike. So the same share price at one-month maturity would generate profits, whereas on a set date it would produce losses. This is fundamentally owing to the option's temporary value, which is of particular significance in contexts of elevated volatility.

In general, the price of the structure at any moment can be expressed as follows:

Call warrant price

$$= \frac{\text{call(underlying, strike, volatility, rate, dividend, time)} \times \text{number of warrants}}{\text{factor of participation}}$$

Put warrant price

$$= \frac{\text{put(underlying, strike, volatility, rate, dividend, time)} \times \text{number of warrants}}{\text{factor of participation}}$$

4

EQUITY DEPOSIT

Definition and commercial presentation

Equity deposits constitute a structure where the investor profits from a growth in a basic across-the-counter asset, instead of a fixed interest rate. An equity deposit investor will receive interest for investing in it, which will be equal in percentage terms to the appreciation. The appreciation is defined, also in percentage terms, by the asset or reference index at a fixed date in relation to the outset.

It is usual to have maturity dates between short and medium terms, although on certain occasions there may arise structures having a longer time period. Depending on the case involved, the whole principal is guaranteed or only part of it is guaranteed. When guaranteeing the principal alone, only a percentage of the asset's appreciation or reference index is offered. All this is also conditioned by time and market conditions.

$$\text{Payoff} = \max\left(0, \frac{S_f - S_0}{S_0}\right) \times \text{percent initial deposit} \qquad (4.1)$$

where

S_0 = underlying of initial position
S_f = underlying of final position

Figure 4.1 shows the payoff diagram.

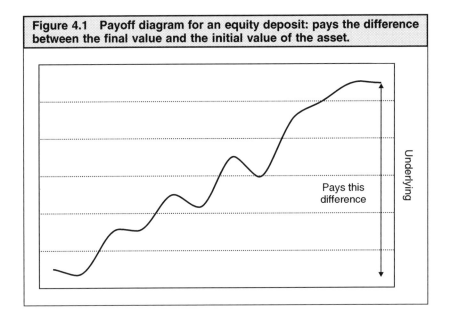

Figure 4.1 Payoff diagram for an equity deposit: pays the difference between the final value and the initial value of the asset.

Risks

This structure defines a basic risk in interest rates, in the direction taken by the underlying, and in volatility.

For the investor

Whoever buys this structure is defining some bullish expectations in the underlying asset. It is expected that the relative growth in the underlying will exceed the risk-free interest rate, which is valid for the term of the structure in question. These are accompanied by some bullish expectations in terms of the particular volatility of the underlying asset.

For the issuer

The profile is the opposite for the issuer. If he does not cover the structure, he will run the risk of paying higher profit levels at interbank deposit interest rate valid at the product launch. Moreover, some harm would be felt, through an increase in volatility of the underlying, since its net position would be as option seller (see later). Eventual reductions in short-term interest rates during the life of the structure would assume it to have a negative cost opportunity, in relative terms, compared to the liability secured through it.

Construction

Construction begins with the issue of a zero coupon deposit, and an underlying asset call option which serves as reference within the structure. The strike is established on the date the operation is agreed; in a case where profitability is offered through growth in the asset since its initial date, it will be equal to how the asset is quoted in the marketplace at the moment of issue. If the underlying would have exceeded the strike on its maturity, the total interest payable to the investor will be the appreciation between the strike and the final underlying.

The investor invests a principal, for which he will only be paid the interest derived from percentage growth in the underlying until maturity. For this, he receives a standard European option from the issuer. So that the issuer can guarantee 100% of the principal to the investor when the structure matures, the option handed to him will have a limited value, owing to the difference between the principal and its present value. This takes into account the interest rate and terms until maturity.

Example

Let's assume a structure where the customer is offered a one-year deposit, in which the appreciation of the reference stock price index (SPI) will be paid, starting at a level of 4000. We shall use the umbrella term SPI, but in reality it could be Nasdaq, Eurostock, Ibex 35, etc. Now let's assume that only 38% of the increase in the SPI will be guaranteed. We will soon see why.

Data items

- Interest rate: 4%
- Dividend: 3%
- Time: 1 year
- Volatility: 25.00%

Indicative terms

Description	Deposit in euros with income linked to an SPI
Nominal	€100 000 000
Issue price	100%
Interest	Variable according to SPI during the operation term; the interest will be equal to 38% of its appreciation between the operation's commencement date and maturity
Term	1 year
Maturity	100% nominal is guaranteed

We need to find the value of a European call with the following characteristics:

- Underlying: 4000
- Strike: 4000
- Time: 1 year
- Rate: 4%
- Dividend: 3%
- Volatility: 25%

In our case this option, valued by Black–Scholes, would be

$$\text{Call} = e^{-qT}SN(d_1) - Ke^{-rT}N(d_2)$$
$$= 2.7182^{-3\% \times 1} \times 4000N(0.165) - 4000$$
$$\times\ 2.7182^{-4\% \times 1}N(-0.085) = 403.843$$

with

$$d_1 = \frac{\ln(4000/4000) + [4\% - 3\% + \frac{1}{2}(25\%)^2] \times 1}{25\% \times \sqrt{1}} = 0.165$$

$$d_2 = 0.165 - 25\% \times \sqrt{1} = -0.085$$

It would cost 403.843 index points, which is 10.096075% of nominal, or €10 096 075.

$$403.843/4000 = 10.096075\%$$

$$10.096\% \times 100\,000\,000 = €10\,096\,075$$

To guarantee a refund of €100 000 000 within one year, its present value must be invested at the outset, i.e. $100\,000\,000/(1 + 4\%) = €96\,153\,846$. This leaves €3 846 154 available to purchase the option. As the option covering the whole increase is worth €10 096 075, appreciation of the SPI can only be offered at a rate of 38.1%:

$$3\,846\,154/10\,096\,075 = 38.09\%$$

Valuation

We need to calculate two quantities for a valuation:

- A deposit until the structure matures
- Standard European call option

The value of a call will be calculated using the Black–Scholes model for dividend-paying assets, conditioned by basic factors quoted in previous chapters.

Having obtained the option value, we must analyse the capital which may be guaranteed as well as the percentage appreciation the investor may be offered. We will start from the fundamental premise that in order to guarantee refund of the same capital (capital$_0$) invested on the maturity date, the structurer or issuer must invest the present value of this capital at the outset, once he receives the capital, as if refund was being made at maturity date. The result is clear: the investment necessary to refund at some future time the same amount as invested today, is its present value. For this, we can say that given an initial capital (capital$_0$) invested by the buyer (the investor), if there is a wish to guarantee at maturity that capital$_T$ = capital$_0$, then the required investment is given by

$$\frac{capital_T}{(1+r)^T} \tag{4.2}$$

where

capital$_T$ = the same capital at a future time T, i.e. at maturity
r = risk-free interest rate
T = time in years

We can also calculate capital − required investment = availability; this is the capital available to invest in options which the issuer will deliver in consideration to the investor. If the option value is greater than this difference, then there are two possibilities:

• Offer the investor a participation percentage in movement of the underlying, lower than the 100%, which would be

$$\frac{availability}{option\ value} \tag{4.3}$$

• Offer 100% participation in movement of the underlying, to avoid the need to guarantee 100% of the capital; the guarantee might be

$$Percentage\ of\ guarantee = \frac{(capital_0 - option\ value) \times (1+r)^T}{capital_0} \tag{4.4}$$

The price of the structure at any moment will be as follows:

Equity deposit price

    = call(underlying, strike, volatility, rate, dividend, time)

       + present value (100% or percentage of the same amount guaranteed)

5

ASIAN DEPOSIT

Definition and commercial presentation

This is a deposit where the investor will obtain interest equal to the average appreciation, determined by the reference asset, during its life, with samples being taken at a rate stipulated in the contract. In structures of this type, which are related to shares or stock price indices, averages are calculated usually at a weekly or monthly rate during the life of the deposit.

The maturity date is usually between short and medium term, although depending on conditions within the principal guaranteed, this may be defined as a longer term. Depending on the case involved, the whole principal is guaranteed or only part of it is guaranteed. When guaranteeing the principal alone, only a percentage of the average asset appreciation is offered. Where the principal is not guaranteed, there is now a trend, especially in the regulations, to avoid the deposit title.

$$\text{Payoff} = \max\left(0, \frac{S_m - S_0}{S_0}\right) \times \text{percent initial deposit} \qquad (5.1)$$

where

S_0 = initial reference asset price
S_m = average reference asset price during the option's life

Figure 5.1 shows the payoff diagram.

Risks

This structure is defined by a basic risk in interest rates, direction of movement of the underlying, and volatility. The sensitivity to volatility is lower than

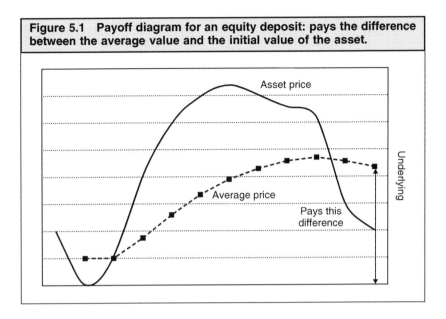

Figure 5.1   Payoff diagram for an equity deposit: pays the difference between the average value and the initial value of the asset.

in structures based on real asset price movement. As a function of a price-averaging income, volatility of the reference index is weakened considerably, although the asset being calculated is naturally highly volatile. Clearly, the frequency with which samples are taken for the average will be of special relevance. Later on we will show that in this type of structure, the so-called Asian options are involved. These are named after their originators. About twenty years ago, options based on averages began to appear in Japan. The Asian option emerged out of the necessity to cover the currency positions of Japanese businesses. The annual reports of these businesses were expressed in accordance with the average exchange rate throughout the year.

The sensitivity of these options to variations in volatility is lower than for standard options of similar life. It would only be equal in the extreme case of daily observation of data for calculating the average. This lesser relative sensitivity of the Asian versions is what justifies the lower cost compared to standard European options. Their lower price improves the profitability conditions of Asian deposits.

For the investor

Whoever buys this structure is defining some bullish expectations of the underlying asset. It is expected that the average relative growth in this will exceed the level of risk-free interest rates, valid for the term of the structure in question. These are accompanied by some moderately bullish expectations in volatility of the underlying asset. The investor reduces risks in temporary falls in reference asset price, in the final stage of the product's life, especially if, until that point, a favourable average has accumulated.

For the issuer

The issuer has the opposite profile. Where he does not cover the structure, he will run the risk of paying income higher than the interbank deposit interest rates at product launch. Even if some harm would be seen through an increase in volatility of the underlying, the effect in terms relative to structurings, based on European options, would be quite minor – as minor as the frequency of data being taken for the average. Temporary reductions in short-term interest rates, during the life of the structure, would suggest a negative opportunity cost, relative to the liability secured through the structure.

Construction

Construction begins with the issue of a zero coupon deposit and an Asian call option, which serves as a reference. The strike is established on the date when the contract is signed. In cases where income is offered through the average asset movement computed from the starting date of the structured product, the strike of the option involved should be the market asset price at that date. If, on maturity, the average would have exceeded the strike, the total interest that the investor must be paid will be the appreciation between this average and the strike price.

A person who invests in an Asian deposit structure invests a principal, through which he will only be paid the interest derived from the percentage growth in the average price of the underlying until maturity. For this, the investor receives from the issuer an Asian option with an agreed data observation frequency. So the issuer may guarantee the investor 100% of the principal when the structure matures, the option handed to him will have a value limited by the difference between the principal and its present value, taking consideration of the interest rate and term until maturity.

Example

Let's assume a structure in which the customer is offered a one-year deposit, starting at a level of 4000, on which the average appreciation of the reference stock price index will be paid. We will call this index SPI. At a monthly rate, index values will be taken to the end of the next 12 months. The percentage difference of that average, with respect to the initial value, will be the interest paid to the investor. Under the same market conditions, defined in the exchange deposit structure, where the principal and an appreciation of 38.2% were guaranteed, we will now analyse the possibilities of this structure.

Data items

- Interest rate: 4%
- Dividend: 3%
- Time: 1 year
- Volatility: 25.00%

Indicative terms

Description	Deposit in euros with income linked to an SPI
Nominal	€100 000 000
Issue price	100%
Interest	Variable according to growth in the monthly average of the SPI during the term of operation. Interest will be equal to a percentage of the average appreciation between the commencement and maturity dates. The average will be calculated at a monthly rate to the end of each month. The percentage will be determined later on
Term	1 year
Maturity	100% nominal is guaranteed

Valuation of this structure requires calculating the Asian call value with the following characteristics:

- Underlying: 4000
- Strike: 4000
- Time: 1 year
- Observations: monthly, at the close of each month or on the following working day (12 observations)
- Rate: 4%
- Dividend: 3%
- Volatility: 25%

In our case this option will be assessed through the Levy approximation, namely, to calculate moments up to the second order:

$$\text{Call} = e^{-rT}[M_1 N(d_1) - KN(d_2)]$$

$$= 2.7182^{-4\% \times 1} \times [4021.755 \times N(0.1122) - 4000 \times N(-0.0041768)]$$

$$= 247.009$$

$$d_1 = \frac{\ln(4021.755/4000) + [\frac{1}{2}(25\%)^2] \times 1}{25\% \times \sqrt{1}} = 0.1122$$

$$d_2 = 0.1122 - 25\% \times \sqrt{1} = -0.0041768$$

$$\sigma = \ln M_2 - 2\ln M_1$$

M_1 is the first-order moment with respect to the average, and M_2 is the second-order moment. In the section on valuation we will set up the calculation model. In our example the two moments have these values:

$$M_1 = 4021.755$$

$$M_2 = 16\,562\,632.59$$

And given the cost of 247.01 index points, namely 6.17748% of nominal or €6 177 475, we have

$$247.009/4000 = 6.17748\%$$

$$6.17748\% \times 100\,000\,000 = €6\,177\,475$$

To guarantee a refund of €100 000 000 within one year, its present value must be invested at the outset, i.e. $100\,000\,000/(1 + 4\%) = €96\,153\,846$. This leaves €3 846 154 available to purchase the option. Since the option value to cover the whole rise is €6 177 475, appreciation of the SPI can be offered at 62.26%:

$$3\,846\,154/6\,177\,475 = 62.26\%$$

Notice that the participation percentage in this type of structure is greater than for a European option, which guarantees a profitability in real terms instead of in average terms. The smaller cost of this type of option allows this greater participation, yet it will also demand that the underlying asset not only has a positive behaviour at the end of the period but also throughout it. As an advantage, remember that a positive reference asset's behaviour during the major part of the structure's life would not be easily offset by a final fall, since its weighting in the total average is much more limited.

Valuation

We will need to calculate these two quantities:

- A zero coupon deposit until maturity of the structure
- A one-year Asian call option with monthly fixings

We can calculate the call value using the Levy approximation model. This technique is based on the hypothesis that the logarithm of the arithmetic average follows a normal distribution. Under this premise, the mean and variance of this normal distribution may be calculated with relative ease using the first two moments of the average. If the average of the asset is calculated, with finite observations, then the two first moments will be given as follows (Hull 2000, pp. 496–98):

$$M_1 = \frac{1}{m} \sum_{i=1}^{m} F_i \tag{5.2}$$

$$P^2 = \frac{1}{m^2} \sum_{i=1}^{m} \sum_{j=1}^{m} S_i S_j \tag{5.3}$$

where
$$E(S_i S_j) = F_i F_j \exp(\rho_{ij} \sigma_i \sigma_j \sqrt{T_i T_j}) \tag{5.4}$$

When $i < j$ we have
$$\rho_{ij} = \frac{\sigma_i \sqrt{T_i}}{\sigma_j \sqrt{T_j}} \tag{5.5}$$

For which
$$E(S_i S_j) = F_i F_j \exp(\sigma_i^2 T_i) \tag{5.6}$$

And therefore
$$M_2 = \frac{1}{m_2} \left[\sum_{i=1}^{m} F_i^2 \exp\left(\sigma_i^2 T_i\right) + 2 \sum_{i<j} F_i F_j \exp\left(\sigma_i^2 T_i\right) \right] \tag{5.7}$$

where

S_i = asset price at moment T_i
F_i = forward asset price at moment T_i
σ_i = implied volatility for asset option at maturity T_i
r_i = correlation between asset profitability, volatility until moment T_i and its profitability until moment T_i
P = arithmetic average
M_1 = first-order moment of P (neutral risk)
M_2 = second-order moment of P (neutral risk)

Even though this technique is widely used, we can generate better valuations by employing an extra parameter. Specifically, alternative models use a lognormal distribution based on the fact that the average, or rather a bias, improves the calculation of the Asian option value. This bias is the asymmetry, for which we need the third-order moment of P. This is particularly relevant when the option is very long term, or when there are very elevated levels of implied volatility quoted in the market for the underlying; this could happen with index options or shares taken out in the technology sector.

To guarantee refund of the same capital invested (capital$_0$) when the operation reaches maturity, the issuer, once he receives the capital, must invest its present value, as if it were being refunded on maturity. For this, it must be kept in mind that, given an initial capital (capital$_0$), invested by the buyer (investor), if there is a wish to guarantee that, on maturity, capital$_T$ = capital$_0$, then the required investment is

$$\frac{\text{capital}_T}{(1+r)^T} \tag{5.8}$$

where

capital$_T$ = the same capital at a future time T, i.e. at maturity
r = risk-free interest rate
T = time in years

The availability is obtained by taking the capital and subtracting the required investment; it is the capital available for investment in the options, which the issuer will hand over to the investor in consideration. If the option value is greater than this difference, then there are two possibilities:

• Offer the investor a participation percentage in the movement of the underlying, lower than 100%, which would be

$$\frac{\text{availability}}{\text{option value}} \tag{5.9}$$

• Offer 100% participation in movement of the underlying, at the expense of not guaranteeing 100% of the capital; the guarantee might be

$$\text{Percentage of guarantee} = \frac{(\text{capital}_0 - \text{option value}) \times (1+r)^T}{\text{capital}_0} \tag{5.10}$$

When comparing a deposit based on a European option and an Asian option, where equal market conditions exist, the Asian option will offer a greater participation or better guarantee conditions. For this, these structured products are recommendable for the more conservative investors since they will not be so demanding in terms of profitability, with respect to other possibilities.

The price of the structure at any moment will be given by

Asian deposit price =

    call(underlying, strike, volatility, rate, dividend, time, frequency)

    + present value (100% or percentage of this principal guaranteed)

6

STRADDLE WITH KNOCKOUT DEPOSIT

Definition and commercial presentation

The straddle with knockout deposit is a structure with guaranteed principal and variable coupon associated with movement in a share or reference stock price index. The special feature is rooted in offering a positive profitability if the reference asset does not remain stable, or does not fall significantly. In these cases the investor would not obtain positive profitability, although he would recover his investment. Profitability of investment is maximised only when the reference asset rises to determined levels which, even where they are exceeded, would generate lower profitability.

Usually the maturity date is between short and medium term and the principal is guaranteed.

$$\text{Payoff} = 0\%\Big|_{S_1 < aS_0} , \max\left(\text{absolute value}\left(\frac{S_f - S_0}{S_0}\right)\right)\Big|_{aS_0 < S_f < bS_0} , F\%$$

(6.1)

where

S_0 = underlying at initial time
S_f = underlying at final time
a = percentage lower than 100% representative of the lower fall limit

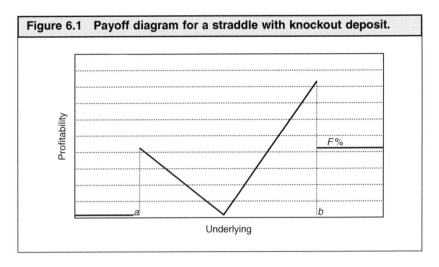

Figure 6.1 Payoff diagram for a straddle with knockout deposit.

b = percentage higher than 100% representative of the upper rise limit
$F\%$ = fixed profitability

Figure 6.1 shows the payoff diagram.

Risks

This structure is determined by a basic risk in interest rates, direction of movement of the underlying, and volatility.

For the investor

Whoever buys this structure is defining moderately bullish expectations of the underlying asset with respect to the initial value. It is expected that the relative growth in the asset will exceed the risk-free interest level valid for the structure's term. However, this will be up to a certain limit, once the structure offers a fixed profitability lower than the variable maximum, which can be reached for more important rises in the underlying. Falls in the underlying might even allow greater relative profitability, although within limits under which the structure does not generate profitability. The person buying this structure must consistently have bullish expectations about the volatility of the underlying asset.

For the issuer

The profile is the opposite for the issuer. If the structure were not covered, the issuer would run the risk of paying higher profitability than the interbank deposit interest rates valid at the moment of issue. Moreover, there would be some harm from an increase in volatility of the underlying, which might not be capable of finally taking this far from the initial level. In fact, there are three zones in which an uncovered issuer will optimise the issue:

- Final stability of the underlying when it matures
- Significant falls in the underlying
- Significant rises in the underlying

Eventual reductions in short-term interest rates during the life of the structure would also suggest a negative opportunity cost, relative to the liability secured.

Construction

Construction begins with the issue of a zero coupon deposit, an at-the-money (ATM) knockout barrier put option and an ATM knockout barrier call option with rebate. The two options have distinct barrier levels and disabling.

A knockout barrier option is an option whose survival depends on the special underlying asset not reaching a determined level. If it does, then the option disappears, leaving its holder with no possible strike, and in the best case granting him the right to cash in a fixed compensation called *rebate*, if this has been agreed within the option. Where this level of option disabling is never reached during its life, then the strike will be the same as for a traditional European option. This is where the positive difference between strike and the underlying asset's final price will be turned into liquid funds, leaving the position at the money.

The structure is incorporated within a so-called straddle (purchase of a call and put with the same strike) of two barrier options, which is handed to the investor. Moreover, the investor has a zero coupon deposit with the issuer, for a nominal equal to the present value in ready cash invested in such a way that, in the worst case, he will recover his investment without interest at maturity. The difference between the straddle's call and put is that the put has a barrier level lower than the current price of the underlying, whereas the call is above this level. In addition, the put does not incorporate rebate within this structure; where the holder is disabled, the put would collect nothing whereas the call would collect something.

In short, an investor who invests in a straddle with knockout deposit lends a principal, for which he is paid the interest derived from the variation (upturn or downturn) of the underlying within a determined range. Outside of this, nothing will be collected beneath it, and above it an income will be collected that is relatively lower than for a risk-free asset of the same term. For this, he receives from the issuer a knockout with spot barrier put, strike at the money (equal to the initial underlying) with barrier level at strike $a\%$ (lower than 100%).

Moreover, he also receives a knockout with strike at the money spot barrier call (equal to the underlying) with barrier level at strike $b\%$ (higher than 100%) and rebate $F\%$ (lower than standard deposit market interest rate for the term in question). So that the issuer may guarantee the investor 100% of the principal when the structure matures, the option handed to him will have a value limited by the difference between the principal and its present value, taking into consideration the interest rate and term until maturity.

Example

Let's assume a structure where the investor is offered a one-year deposit, starting at a level of 4000, in which he will be paid the variation (positive or negative) with reference to a stock price index (SPI) as long as this does not fall more than 24.5% or rise more than 16%. Where the SPI might increase by more than 16%, the investor will only receive 2%. The principal is guaranteed.

Indicative terms

Description	Deposit in euros with income linked to an SPI
Nominal	€100 000 000
Issue price	100%
Interest	Variable with respect to growth in SPI during term of operation. Interest will be equal to net variation in SPI with respect to the starting level of 4000 within a range of 3020 and 4640 (in absolute value, for which income within the range is always positive, independent of whatever rise or fall there may be in range). If the SPI falls below 3020 then the investor will receive nothing. If it exceeds 4640 then the investor collects 2%
Term	1 year
Maturity	100% nominal is guaranteed

To carry out a valuation, we will need to calculate these three quantities:

- A down-and-out 4000 put with barrier at 3020 (24.5% fall from 4000)
- An up-and-out 4000 call with barrier at 4640 (16% rise from 4000)
- Rebate of 80 points (2%)

The valuation is carried out using the following information:

- Underlying: 4000
- Time: 1 year

- Risk-free rate: 4%
- Dividend: 3%
- Volatility: 25%

The volatility is the same for both call and put, from which we are omitting smiles or spreads from volatility. In our example we will obtain the following costs by valuing the barrier options under the Black–Scholes framework:

- Down-and-out put: 94.88 points (2.37%)
- Up-and-out call: 53.79 points (1.34%)
- Total: 3.72%

To be able to refund the principal of €10 000 000 at year end, the issuer must initially invest its present value of 4%, namely, €9 615 385 in a deposit. Therefore the maximum option value the issuer will hand the investor so as not to experience a loss position during the operation, is limited to €384 615 (3.85%). If the options handed over are worth €371 679 (3.72%), the issuer's margin will be reduced to the difference, which in this case is barely 0.13% of nominal.

Valuation

We need to calculate these three quantities:

- A deposit until the structure matures, with principal at present value of the initial investment
- Down-and-out put option (DO)
- Up-and-out call option (UO) with rebate

The valuation model for the barriers is given by these variables:

- *Price of underlying asset*: asset market price, for which the option is nominated
- *Option strike price*: price of purchase (call) or sale (put) agreed on the option
- *Barrier price*: for knockouts this is the level at which if it is rising through the underlying asset price, during the option's life, then the underlying asset price disappears
- *Implied volatility*: volatility quoted in the market, which the market assigns implicitly and potentially to future increases in underlying asset price for the option's life
- *Risk-free interest rate*: market interest rate, corresponding to existing term between date of valuation and option maturity

- *Dividends paid by the underlying asset*: dividends chargeable to the asset for which the option is nominated during its life. This is expressed as a continuous annualised interest rate
- *Time to option maturity*: time expressed in years between the valuation date and maturity

Here are the analytical formulae for valuing barrier options within the Black–Scholes framework:

$$A = \phi S e^{(b-r)T} N(\phi d_1) - \phi K e^{-rT} N(\phi d_1 - \phi \sigma \sqrt{T}) \tag{6.2}$$

$$B = \phi S e^{(b-r)T} N(\phi d_3) - \phi K e^{-rT} N(\phi d_3 - \phi \sigma \sqrt{T}) \tag{6.3}$$

$$C = \phi S e^{(b-r)T} (H/S)^{2(\mu+1)} N(\eta d_5) - \phi K e^{-rT} (H/S)^{2\mu} N(\eta d_5 - \eta \sigma \sqrt{T}) \tag{6.4}$$

$$D = \phi S e^{(b-r)T} (H/S)^{2(\mu+1)} N(\eta d_7) - \phi K e^{-rT} (H/S)^{2\mu} N(\eta d_7 - \eta \sigma \sqrt{T}) \tag{6.5}$$

$$E = R e^{rT} [N(\eta d_3 - \eta \sigma \sqrt{T}) - (H/S)^{2\mu} N(\eta d_7 - \eta \sigma \sqrt{T})] \tag{6.6}$$

$$F = R e^{rT} [(H/S)^{\mu+\lambda} N(\eta d_9) + (H/S)^{\mu-\lambda} N(\eta d_9 - 2\eta \lambda \sigma \sqrt{T})] \tag{6.7}$$

where

S = price of underlying
K = strike price
H = barrier level
R = rebate
σ = volatility
r = risk-free interest rate
b = net cost of carry = $r - q$
q = dividends
T = time
η = 1 for down and −1 for up
ϕ = 1 for call and −1 for put

$$d_1 = \frac{\ln(S/K)}{\sigma \sqrt{T}} + (1 + \mu)\sigma \sqrt{T} \quad d_3 = \frac{\ln(S/H)}{\sigma \sqrt{T}} + (1 + \mu)\sigma \sqrt{T}$$

$$d_5 = \frac{\ln(H^2/SK)}{\sigma \sqrt{T}} + (1 + \mu)\sigma \sqrt{T} \quad d_7 = \frac{\ln(H/S)}{\sigma \sqrt{T}} + (1 + \mu)\sigma \sqrt{T}$$

$$d_9 = \frac{\ln(H/S)}{\sigma \sqrt{T}} + \lambda \sigma \sqrt{T} \quad \mu = \frac{b - \sigma^2/2}{\sigma \sqrt{T}} \quad \lambda = \sqrt{\mu^2 + 2r/\sigma^2}$$

The various barrier options will be given as follows:

Call DO $(K > H) = A - C + F$	$\eta = 1$	$\phi = 1$	(6.8)
Call DO $(K < H) = B - D + F$	$\eta = 1$	$\phi = 1$	(6.9)
Call UO $(K > H) = F$	$\eta = -1$	$\phi = 1$	(6.10)
Call UO $(K < H) = A - B + C - D + F$	$\eta = -1$	$\phi = 1$	(6.11)
Put DO $(K > H) = A - B + C - D + F$	$\eta = 1$	$\phi = -1$	(6.12)
Put DO $(K < H) = F$	$\eta = 1$	$\phi = -1$	(6.13)
Put UO $(K > H) = B - D + F$	$\eta = -1$	$\phi = -1$	(6.14)
Put UO $(K < H) = A - C + F$	$\eta = -1$	$\phi = -1$	(6.15)

These price variations in the underlying are like a variable following a Brownian process under a normal distribution. This is relevant for determining final price and range, in relation to barrier levels. To find its path, we need not only its final value but also the instantaneous probability that the barrier level may rise. Equations (6.6) and (6.7) include the rebate when the barrier is reached.

The price of the structure at any moment is given by

Straddle with knockout price =

call UO(underlying, strike, barrier, volatility, rate, dividend, time, rebate)

+ put DO(underlying, strike, barrier, volatility, rate, dividend, time)

+ the principal's present value

7
DIGITAL RANGES

Definition and commercial presentation

Digital ranges are also called accrual notes, corridor notes and hamster. Hamster is an acronym which has come to signify 'hope for a market stabilisation in a given range'. This chapter looks at digital ranges linked to equity assets; Chapter 16 looks at digital ranges linked to interest rates.

This type of structure potentially offers the investor higher than market interest. Even if this interest is paid when the operation matures, it is accrued and calculated on a daily basis, whenever an index, defined as reference within the structure – for equity this means any reference stock price index (SPI) – is situated in a range which will have been defined by the investor when the operation started. The only restriction imposed by the issuer is the bandwidth. The investor may position this where he wants for the life of the investment.

In short, we are dealing with a structure where the principal is guaranteed and the final interest depends on the investor's level of success with the evolution of a reference index within a predefined range. This is restricted by the width rather than its relative position. Commercially, a structure is offered that pays out interest higher than the market rate, accrued daily, whenever the reference index is positioned within a previously defined band. If this does not occur, then no interest is paid or nominal amounts are paid, traditionally called *rebate*, in respect of market conditions.

The maturity date is usually short term, about a year, and is issued by guaranteeing the principal.

$$\text{Payoff} = \max(0, D_{\text{success}} \times r_x/365) \qquad (7.1a)$$

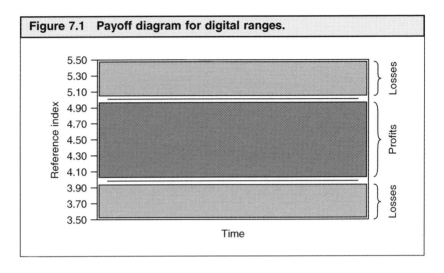

Figure 7.1   Payoff diagram for digital ranges.

or alternatively

$$\text{Payoff} = D_{\text{success}} \times \frac{r_x}{365} + (D_{\text{total}} - D_{\text{success}}) \times \frac{\text{rebate}}{365} \qquad (7.1b)$$

Figure 7.1 shows the payoff diagram.

Risks

This structure is determined by a basic risk in interest rates and volatility. The inherent risk differs from an investment, which is a fundamental substitute, like a standard deposit, where stability in the reference index (an asset of another financial type such as an equity) favours obtaining greater levels in profitability. In the same way, movement in interest rates has an effect on this type of structure – a predominantly negative effect. That is to say, interest rate rises will have a downward effect on the structure's market value. On the one hand, as we shall see, the structure's value will require us to calculate the present value of the interest already accrued. Increases in the rate of revaluation will imply a lower price. On the other hand, rises in standard alternative investment rates, free from risk of volatility (a standard deposit), will assume a greater opportunity cost for these structures.

For the investor

Whoever buys this structure is defining expectations for a stable underlying asset, in this case stock price index assets represented by any SPI. Maximisation of profits occurs where prices are stable or the index value is within the predefined range. By virtue of this, the investor adopts a position to sell the volatility within this structure. Therefore, the risk emerges in volatile situations, which take the reference index outside the band predefined by the investor when the operation starts.

For the issuer

The risk for the issuer comes from a stable scenario. Finally, where he does not cover the structure, the issuer has a speculative position as 'buyer in volatility' and would suffer harm at the end of the operation if, during its life, the reference index were to remain stable within the range. Financially speaking, in this case the options in favour of the issuer would end up by expiring out of the money (OTM) – without value. Finally, the issuer would end up paying a rate higher than market rate.

Construction

In spite of all appearances to the contrary – very common with structures – the issuer of an equity corridor note takes from the investor a deposit at a rate of interest r_x, higher than the market rate r_m, at the moment he receives from the investor some digital options. In fact, for the investor, the structure is a deposit which has an extra rate $r_x - r_m$, and this should therefore be accounted for. To do that, the investor should consider these two options:

- Digital calls with strike equal to the higher band level chosen by the investor, and

$$\text{Payoff} = \frac{r_x}{365} \times \text{nominal}$$

- Digital puts with strike equal to the lower band level chosen by the investor, and

$$\text{Payoff} = \frac{r_x}{365} \times \text{nominal}$$

The numbers of calls and puts will be given by the working days over which the interest is computed during the investment period. For example, for one year there will be approximately 250 calls and 250 puts.

When the principal for the nominal received is all that is guaranteed, then only the present value of this nominal must be invested so that, when the structure matures, the same principal will be obtained over that period as the amount the investor handed over at the outset.

Where the issuer offers the investor a consolation return, or rebate, for each day the reference index falls outside the band, the structure will incorporate a 'set' of 250 other digital calls and 250 digital puts (per year). Now, these options will be in favour of the investor, with daily payoff (for liquid capital on maturity) equal to this rebate. In this way, in the total structure (per year) there will be 500 options in favour of the issuer with payoff equal to the rate offered on the structure, and 500 options in favour of the investor with payoff equal to the rebate.

Example

Let's assume that a corridor note structure offers 5.50% (its share proportional to each of the 365 days invested) for each day on which the reference stock price index, e.g. Ibex 35, is situated within a maximum band of 500 points, whenever the investor wishes. Let's assume a current Ibex 35 value of 11 000. For each day on which the reference index is outside the band, the investor will accrue 0% interest. The market interest rate of a standard deposit is 4.5%. The investor chooses where to position the predicted fluctuation band, according to future Ibex 35 expectations, on each day throughout the investment period. Final liquidation of interest will occur when the operation matures (after one year).

Indicative terms

Description	Deposit in euros with high return linked to Ibex 35
Nominal	€10 000 000
Issue price	100%
Interest	5.50% daily for each day the Ibex 35 index is within a band set in advance by the customer when the operation starts. Maximum bandwidth will be 500 points. Whenever the index is outside this band, 0% interest will accrue on any such day. Successes and errors made on Fridays will be calculated for 3 days. The interest accumulated is paid on maturity
Term	1 year
Maturity	100%

Let's assume that the investor chooses to position the band in the range 10 750–11 250 (very central in terms of current levels) and invests €10 million nominal. Hypothetically, the issuer receives, on the investor's structure, 250 digital calls at 11 250 with payoff 5.50%/365 and 250 digital puts at 10 750 with the same payoff. Maturity dates for each of the 250 calls and puts correspond to each of the future days on which the index position will be assessed in respect of the bands chosen. This means all working days from start-up to one year ahead. Where the index is positioned within strikes, the investor would consolidate the 5.50%, or equally, the options in favour of the issuer would expire out of the money.

Where the index is positioned above or below the band limits, the issuer would exercise his options on a daily basis, and take his return from the structure. Taken to an extreme (the index is below or above the bands), then from the first day of investment to the last day of investment, exercising all these options would bring the issuer 5.50% over 365 days, which would be the interest that the investor would not be receiving. This is the case where the investor would finally obtain the nominal invested.

Looking at how the issuer handles this position, with the nominal received at 100%, he will have to invest the present value of the nominal at 365 day market interest rate, which in our example is $10\,000\,000/(1 + 4.50\%) = €9\,569\,378$. The objective of this operation is to hedge the interest rate risk of the deposit taken, or finally, to insure himself so that in one year he will get the principal which has to be returned to the investor. Remembering that the issuer assumes a risk for the underlying and volatility, for which at maturity, where the investor has had success within the bands he has set, the issuer will have to assume payment of interest higher than market level. There is the possibility that the issuer will choose to handle or cancel this risk.

A clear success in the bands set by the investor would assume that the options obtained by the issuer would have expired out of the money. The simplest way for the issuer to cancel or close this risk would be to sell the 250 digital calls and 250 digital puts with payoff at 5.50%/365, received from the investor, on the market at the outset. Clearly, strikes should be the same: 11 250 for calls and 10 750 for puts. So, where the investor is successful in the chosen bands, the negative effect of the expired out-of-the-money (OTM) options for the issuer would be compensated by the net income from the options sold on the market, which would be exercised for him.

Logically, the underlying of the options should also be Ibex forwards for each of the following 365 days of the year. The issuer would sell the options he receives from the investor to close out his risk in the underlying. The business of the issuer in this case, where the risk is being closed out, is to sell the options obtained at a value higher than the value implicit in the structure he is selling to the customer. The issuer will finance these options using that part of the nominal remaining from investment in the standard deposit. In our case, $100 - 95.69 = 4.31\%$ would be the maximum ready cash available for purchasing the options. In reality, the issuer's profit could be given by the possibility of buying these options at a lower percentage than 4.31%.

Valuation

Valuation of the structure's components is reduced to an interbank deposit at a rate higher than market rate, r_x, along with digital options. Digital options may be European options, whose final payoff is given by a preset quantity rather than by the difference between the final underlying asset and the strike price (call), or vice versa (put). We can follow an analysis based on the Black–Scholes framework. Given the option profile, which has no bearing on the relationship between the underlying strike and the final payoff decision, where in the money (ITM) expires, it is possible to assess the digital options. In valuating the call and the put, it will only be relevant to quantify the strike probability applied to the payoff for the digital option:

$$\text{Call} = Xe^{-rT}N(d) \tag{7.2}$$

$$\text{Put} = Xe^{-rT}N(-d) \tag{7.3}$$

with

$$d = \frac{\ln(S/K) + (r - q + \frac{1}{2}\sigma^2)T}{\sigma\sqrt{T}}$$

where

S = underlying price
K = strike
X = payoff
σ = volatility
r = risk-free interest rate
q = dividend
T = time to option maturity in years

These equations will require a small adjustment. The model assumes the payoff turns into ready cash (where ITM expires) when the option matures. In the structure, all payoffs in all options turn into ready cash when the structure matures. This means we must take Xe^{-rT} and multiply it by e^{zT_f} where z is the interest rate that applies to the existing period between the option maturity date and the structure. Within the structure, the issuer implicitly receives options, in exchange for which he issues a deposit with an extra charge rate $r_x - r_m$.

In a position of financial equilibrium, at the moment the structure is created, the spread over market rates promised by the issuer to the investor only in case of a successful movement of the index inside the band, must be equal to the value of the 500 digital options, implicitly received by the issuer.

Consequently, assessment of this structure, at market prices, is reduced to finding the value in the offered extra rate where there is success every day (remember that interest is paid at the end of the period), and the value of the 250 digital calls (with higher-limit strike) and 250 digital puts (with lower-limit strike) with fixed payoff equal to rate r_x is offered on the structure. At the outset, these options owe value equal to the value in the extra rate:

$$r_x - r_m = \sum_{i=1}^{n} \left[\underset{\text{payoff} = r_x/365}{\text{digital call } (K = \text{higher limit})} + \underset{\text{payoff} = r_x/365}{\text{digital puts } (K = \text{lower limit})} \right]$$

where n is the number of working days during the life of the structure. We must take into account that, even if n is the number of working days, the payoff corresponding to Fridays will be $3r_x/365$, applied to the nominal.

To complete the valuation, we must look at the fundamental risk parameters of Chapter 2: delta and vega.

Delta: sensitivity to the underlying asset price variations

$$\text{Delta for a digital call} = \frac{1}{\sigma S \sqrt{T}} \exp(-rT) \frac{1}{\sqrt{2\pi}} \exp(-d_2^2/2) \qquad (7.4)$$

$$\text{Delta for a digital put} = -\frac{1}{\sigma S \sqrt{T}} \exp(-rT) \frac{1}{\sqrt{2\pi}} \exp(-d_2^2/2) \qquad (7.5)$$

Vega: sensitivity to implied volatility variations

$$\text{Vega for a digital call} = -\exp(-rT) \frac{1}{\sqrt{2\pi}} \exp(-d_2^2/2)(\sqrt{T} + d_2/\sigma) \qquad (7.6)$$

$$\text{Vega for a digital put} = \exp(-rT) \frac{1}{\sqrt{2\pi}} \exp(-d_2^2/2)(\sqrt{T} + d_2/\sigma) \qquad (7.7)$$

The price of the structure at any moment will be given by

$$\text{Price} = \text{present value}(1 + r_x)$$

$$- \sum_{i=1}^{n} \left[\underset{\text{payoff} = r_x/365}{\text{digital call } (K = \text{higher limit})} + \underset{\text{payoff} = r_x/365}{\text{digital puts } (K = \text{lower limit})} \right]$$

$$+ \sum_{i=1}^{n} \left[\underset{\text{payoff} = r_{\text{rebate}}/365}{\text{digital call } (K = \text{higher limit})} + \underset{\text{payoff} = r_{\text{rebate}}/365}{\text{digital puts } (K = \text{lower limit})} \right]$$

$$- \text{present value} \left(\frac{(r_x - r_{\text{rebate}}) \times \text{days observed outside band}}{365} \right)$$

8

REVERSE
CONVERTIBLE

Definition and commercial presentation

This is a structure where the investor may have the potential to obtain a return higher than market return whenever a reference asset is maintained above a determined price. In exchange, the investor takes on the risk of receiving at maturity the same underlying asset to which the operation is linked, where the price of the underlying asset falls below this level. That is, the investor runs the risk at maturity of receiving from the issuer a fixed number of shares to which the structure is tied, instead of obtaining the capital invested originally.

The number of shares corresponds to the nominal invested divided by the share price at the outset. If the share were to fall below the threshold defined in the structure, and therefore at maturity the investor were to receive shares instead of the initial capital, the value of these shares would clearly be lower than this capital, since it would be the number of shares set at source but at a price lower than at that time. Maturity date is usually short to medium term and the principal is not guaranteed in cases of fixed interest reverse and variable nominal.

$$\text{Payoff} = \begin{cases} K - S_f & \text{if } S_f < K \\ X & \text{if } S_f > K \end{cases} \tag{8.1}$$

where

S_0 = underlying of initial position
S_f = underlying of final position
X = fixed amount $\approx$ put sold by issuer > market return

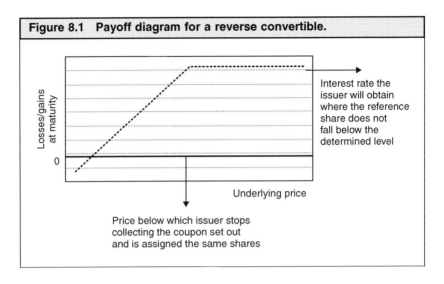

Figure 8.1   Payoff diagram for a reverse convertible.

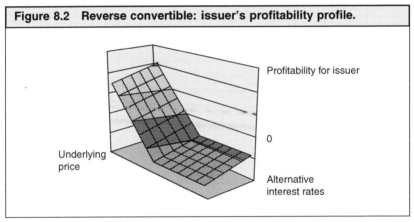

Figure 8.2   Reverse convertible: issuer's profitability profile.

Figure 8.1 shows the payoff diagram.

Risks

This structure is defined by a basic risk in interest rates, the direction of movement of the underlying, and volatility.

For the investor

Whoever buys this structure is determining moderately bullish expectations for the underlying asset. It is expected that the relative growth in this asset will not exceed, in percentage terms, the level of fixed return that would be received where no fall below a determined threshold occurred. These are accompanied by some bearish expectations in terms of the actual volatility of the underlying asset. Maximisation of relative profits occurs in a context where the underlying asset is stable and there has been downward movement in interest rates.

For the issuer

The issuer has the opposite profile (Figure 8.2). If the structure were not covered, the issuer would run the risk of finally paying higher than market returns at the moment of issue. This occurs where there are moderate rises in the underlying asset price, or this price is stable at the issue time. Where the issuer holds a buying position on a put, then the fundamental risk is limited to the premium paid explicitly or implicitly. For the opposite case, this premium is the fixed interest rate offered to the investor where the reference asset at maturity does not fall below the pre-established level. A put position has unlimited potential for profit. In the reverse, when the reference asset matures, the greater the fall in price below the established price, the greater the profit obtained by the issuer in having the right to sell, or deliver, that asset to the investor at the given level.

Construction

The construction of this structure is reduced to a zero coupon for deposit on the part of the investor, who assumes an irrevocable order of purchase of the underlying at a determined price (strike). With this, the investor will obtain the interest agreed and the principal, if the underlying asset is maintained above the strike; in the opposite case, he will receive these titles (instead of the original investment) and the interest.

   This structure allows the issuer to receive financing by paying for a nominally higher than market interest at the time when a put option is received implicitly from the investor. In reality, the valuation of that put allows the issuer to have an effective rate of financing, lower than market level, where hedging has been taken out for the position of taking on funds. If the issuer valuates the option received from the investor lower than the theoretical 'market price', then he would be paying a spread below market interest rates rather than a higher one.

Example

Let's assume a structure where the customer is offered a one-year deposit in dollars. He will be paid a rate higher than market rate (a one-year rate for a market deposit is 7.30%), whenever the reference stock price index (SPI) is located above the 4000 starting level (let's assume this is the current price). Where the SPI might, within a year, be below the initial level, the customer would receive the stated coupon, although instead of the monetary principal, he would be given a basket of shares representative of this coupon at market price when it matures, for the nominal invested. Therefore, he collects the loss in index value on the principal.

Data items

- Initial investment: $100 000
- Interest rate: 7.30%
- Dividend: 4%
- Time to maturity: 1 year
- One-year volatility: 55%

Valuation of this structure is reduced to calculating the value of a one-year at-the-money put on the SPI. In our example, the value of the put, using the Black–Scholes model, is 758.3 points in terms of the index, namely 18.95% of the 4000 strike:

$$
\begin{aligned}
\text{Put} &= Ke^{-rT}N(-d_2) - Se^{-qT}N(-d_1) \\
&= 4000 \times 2.7182e^{-7.30\% \times 1} \times N(-0.3350) \\
&\quad - 4000 \times 2.7182^{-4\% \times 1} \times N(0.2150) \\
&= 758.29
\end{aligned}
$$

$$
d_1 = \frac{\ln(4000/4000) + [7.30\% - 4\% + \frac{1}{2}(55\%)^2] \times 1}{55\% \times \sqrt{1}} = 0.3350
$$

$$
d_2 = 0.3350 - 55\% \times \sqrt{1} = -0.2150
$$

This is the amount being paid by the investor to the issuer using an option to obtain a greater relative return in fixed circumstances. Whenever there is total equilibrium, assuming the investor is not going to be 'penalised', then we may see what starting return he should be offered when the SPI does not fall below the starting reference level. Considering that the option value represents 18.95% of the nominal value invested (for eventual delivery of the shares representative of the index, the 4000 index level will correspond to the $100 000 invested), at present value, and considering it is a one-year structure, the issuer of the reverse will receive $100 000 plus $18 950, which might materialise if he takes the option received from the investor and sells it on the market. Within one year, at 7.3%, with an initial nominal of $118 950, there should be $127 641, which would be the maximum amount available to offer the investor, if no fee is charged (an irrational assumption in the real world of the structurer). Under this assumption, the return offered him would be no less than 27.64% per annum.

Indicative terms

Description	Deposit in dollars with high profit return, linked to an SPI
Nominal	$100 000
Issue price	100%
Interest	27.64%
Term	1 year
Maturity	$100\% \times \min\left[1, \text{SPI}_{+1 \text{ year}}/\text{SPI}_{\text{today}}\right]$

Valuation

We need to calculate these two quantities:

- A deposit until the structure of the nominal matures
- A European put option

Considering that the option is for the issuer and against the investor (the investor delivers the put to the issuer), then to find the value of the whole structure, we must take the option price at present value and subtract it from the nominal and interests of the reverse. Under the Black–Scholes framework, the value of a share put, or stock price indices, is given by six basic factors:

- *Price of the underlying asset*: asset market price at which the option is nominated
- *Price of exercising an option*: purchase price (call) or sale (put) agreed on the option
- *Implied volatility*: volatility quoted in the market, which the market assigns implicitly and potentially to future price movement in the underlying asset for the life of the option
- *Risk-free interest rate*: market interest rate corresponding to the existing term between valuation and maturity dates of the option
- *Dividends paid for by the underlying asset*: dividends attributable to the asset, at which the option is nominated, during the option's life, expressed at a continuous rate of annual interest
- *Time to option maturity*: fraction of a year between dates of valuation and maturity

$$\text{Put} = -e^{-qT}SN(-d_1) + Ke^{-rT}N(-d_2)$$

$$d_1 = \frac{\ln(S/K) + (r - q + \frac{1}{2}\sigma^2)T}{\sigma\sqrt{T}}$$

$$d_2 = d_1 - \sigma\sqrt{T}$$

$$q = -(1/T)\ln\left[1 - \text{PV(dividends)}/S\right]$$

S = price of the underlying
K = strike
σ = volatility
r = risk-free interest rate
q = continuous dividend yield
T = time in years until option matures

and PV(dividends) is the present value of future dividend payments. The price of the structure at any moment before it matures is given by

Reverse price = present value(original nominal + interests of the structure)

$$- \frac{\text{put}_{\text{current value}}(\text{underlying, strike, volatility, rate, dividend, time})}{\text{current underlying} \times \text{nominal}}$$

9

LADDER BOND

Definition and commercial presentation

The ladder bond structure is constructed with options composed of options. The investor in a ladder bond receives interest on his investment; this interest will be positive whenever the reference index reaches determined levels of consolidation which, where successful, will guarantee a return independent of the final position index position on the date the structure matures.

The maturity date is usually short to medium term and, according to the term, the principal is guaranteed in full or only in part.

$$\text{Payoff} = \max\left(0, \frac{L_n - S_0}{S_0}, \frac{S_f - S_0}{S_0}\right) \times \text{ percent initial deposit} \qquad (9.1)$$

where

L_n = ladder consolidation level at intermediate position n
S_0 = underlying of initial position
S_f = underlying of final position

Figure 9.1 shows the payoff diagram.

Risks

This structure is defined by a basic risk in interest rates, direction taken by the underlying, and volatility. It incorporates a ladder option, which in turn may be split into knockout barrier options, similar to those in Chapter 6. A ladder option is an option which allows the holder to consolidate gains generated by the underlying throughout its life, and independent of how

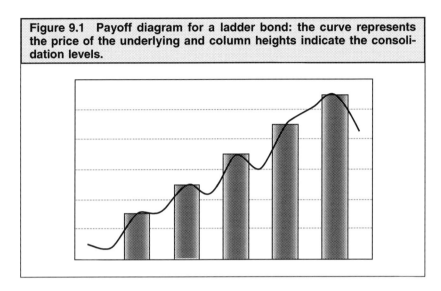

Figure 9.1   Payoff diagram for a ladder bond: the curve represents the price of the underlying and column heights indicate the consolidation levels.

the underlying ends up when the option matures. Considering these special features, the more levels involved in the consolidation, the greater the option cost, hence the greater the structure cost. Figure 9.2 shows the sensitivity of the risks in relation to the underlying for a knockout call option with strike 4000 (SPI type), a barrier level at 4200, and rebate 200 (amount

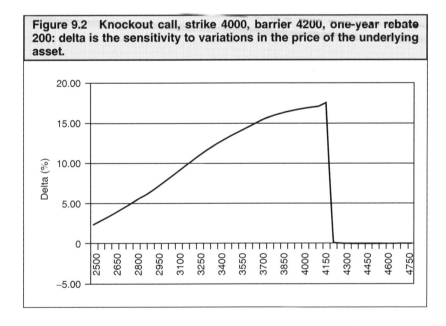

Figure 9.2   Knockout call, strike 4000, barrier 4200, one-year rebate 200: delta is the sensitivity to variations in the price of the underlying asset.

received by the option buyer if the underlying reaches the disabling level and disappears). Notice how the graph is rather erratic. Sensitivity of knockout options, and therefore ladders, is heavily determined by barrier level. When the underlying asset price comes near to the barrier level, the structure will exhibit price instability.

For the investor

Whoever buys this structure is determining some bullish expectations in the underlying asset. It is expected that the relative growth in the underlying asset will exceed the risk-free interest rate valid for the term of the structure. These are accompanied by some bullish expectations in terms of the particular volatility of the underlying asset. Maximisation of the relative profits occurs where there is volatility which allows consolidation levels to rise, even when there are later falls in the underlying asset price. This starts with interest rates in a downward trend.

For the issuer

The issuer has the opposite profile. If the issuer were not to take out cover, he would run the risk of paying higher than market returns at the moment of issue. This is where there are price rises in the underlying asset which allow for some significant levels of consolidated growth. Considering that the growth levels will determine the structure's profitability, independent of a final clear fall in underlying price through a rise in consolidation levels, then the basic risk to the issuer is given by a bullish price movement in the reference underlying asset.

Construction

Construction reduces to a zero coupon deposit and a ladder option. These options are characterised by having a payoff that keeps consolidating in-the-money levels reached throughout its life, in connection with its final liquidation at maturity. On the date when the deal is agreed, the strike and the ladder levels are established in the structure, or rather the progressive levels for consolidating the appreciation. On each working day of the deal's life, observations are carried out on how the reference index is being quoted and the ladders are being recorded, ladders which might have risen in the appropriate circumstances. The positive difference between this value and the strike will be certain profit for the buyer when the option matures. This is independent of the level of the underlying asset at that moment.

If the underlying might even have exceeded the greater of the ladders on this date, then the total profit for the buyer would be given by the appreciation between the strike and this ladder maximum, plus the relative appreciation between this ladder maximum and the final underlying. The payoff profile of these options makes them quite a lot more expensive than other types of exotic option.

There is an exact parity between the ladder options and the barrier option combination of knockouts and European types. Specifically, the value of a call ladder is equal to the same amount of up-and-out calls as ladder levels or consolidation levels. Moreover, each up-and-out call will have a rebate equal to the difference between its strike and the one immediately below it. The European call will have as its strike the ladder level or highest consolidation. The highest consolidation is the option whereby if the underlying exceeds all the ladders, the final liquid capital will also incorporate this gain.

A person who invests in a ladder bond structure invests a principal, through which he will only be paid the interest derived from percentage growth in the underlying until it matures. The special feature here is that the increases keep consolidating independent of any subsequent outcome, but depending on the reference index reaching certain levels. For this, the investor receives from the issuer a ladder option. So that the issuer may guarantee the investor the 100% principal when the structure matures, the option he hands over will have a value limited by the difference between the principal and its present value, taking into consideration the market interest rate and term until maturity.

Example

Let's assume a structure where the customer is offered a one-year bond, on which will be paid the reference stock price index (SPI) appreciation. The gains generated may be consolidated if, at any moment during the period, the index reaches levels of 4200, 4500 and 4700 with a starting level of 4000. Moreover, let's assume that only 89.10% of the nominal was guaranteed, so that, out of €100 million invested, if during the year, at any moment, the SPI were to exceed the consolidation levels (ladder), then the investor would ultimately receive €89.1 million.

Data items

- Market interest rate: 4%
- Dividend: 3%
- Time to maturity: 1 year

Volatilities

- 25.0% (strike 4000)
- 24.5% (strike 4200)

- 24.0% (strike 4500)
- 22.3% (strike 4700)

Indicative terms

Description	Bond in euros with profitability for consolidation over the period and linked to an SPI
Nominal	€100 000 000
Issue price	100%
Interest	Variable in relation to movement in SPI during the deal's term. The interest will be equal to its appreciation during the life of the deal, with gains being consolidated at levels of 4200, 4500 and 4700
Term	1 year
Maturity	Only 89.10% of nominal guaranteed

In addition to calculating the corresponding zero coupon deposit, valuation of this structure is reduced to calculating the value of three up-and-out calls and the European type with the following characteristics:

In general

  call UO(underlying, strike, barrier, rebate, volatility, rate, dividend, time)

In particular

  call UO(4000, 4000, 4200, 4200 − 4000, 25%, 4%, 3%, 1)
    + call UO(4000, 4200, 4500, 4500 − 4200, 24.5%, 4%, 3%, 1)
    + call UO(4000, 4500, 4700, 4700 − 4500, 24%, 4%, 3%, 1)
    + European call(4000, 4700, 22.3%, 4%, 3%, 1)

In our example these four options would come to a value of 573, i.e. 14.32% of the 4000 strike. From the nominal received by the issuer, this amount would be earmarked for the options and the rest invested on a one-year risk-free deposit. By investing almost 85.68% of the nominal for one year at 4%, it would leave only 89.10% at the end of the period.

Valuation

We need to calculate these two quantities:

- A deposit until the structure matures
- Ladder option

The value of a ladder option is given by the sum of various barrier options and one European option. To sum up, synthesis of the barrier options yields knockouts with rebate and standard European options. In our example the synthesis for the structure at the moment of its issue is

$$\sum_{j=0}^{n-1} \text{call UO}(S_t, L_j, L_{j+1}, L_j - L_{j+1}, \sigma, r, q, T)$$

$$+ \text{ European call}(F, L_n, \sigma, r, q, T)$$

where

S_t	= spot underlying
L_j	= highest j ladder strike
L_{j+1}	= ladder barrier following j
$L_j - L_{j+1}$	= magnitude of rebate in the case of knockout (deactivating)
L_n	= top ladder level
σ	= implied volatility
r	= risk-free interest rate when option matures
q	= dividend yield per annum
T	= time to maturity in years
F	= forward or future index price

The price of the structure at any moment is given by

Price = present value of interest until maturity + present value

of the principal (100% or a percentage guaranteed)

+ ladder call(underlying, strike, ladders, volatilities,

rate, dividend, time)

Note that where any consolidation level has been reached during the life of the option, the value of the call ladder will be given by

$$\sum_{j=0}^{n-1} \text{call UO }(S_t, L_j, L_{j+1}, L_j - L_{j+1}, \sigma, r, q, T)$$

$$+ \text{ European call}(F, L_n, \sigma, r, q, T) + e^{-rT}(L_{\text{point reached}} - L_{\text{minimum}})$$

10

BASKET BOND

Definition and commercial presentation

The basket bond is where the investor profits from movement in a set of stock market assets. The investor obtains greater advantages through the possibilities of diversification. Their simplicity of construction, valuation and high added value in managing an equity portfolio, make basket bonds among the most well-known structured products.

The investor in a basket bond will receive interest through his investment, which, in percentage terms, will be equal to appreciation of the assets, or reference index, set on a fixed date in relation to the outset.

The maturity date is usually short to medium term, although structures do sometimes have longer terms. Depending on circumstances, the whole principal may be guaranteed or only part of it. Alternatively, in guaranteeing the principal, only a percentage of the basket's appreciation is offered, determined by the term and market conditions.

$$\text{Payoff} = \max\left(0, \frac{C_f - C_0}{C_0}\right) \times \text{percent initial investment} \qquad (10.1)$$

where

C_0 = initial underlying basket price
C_f = final underlying basket price

Figure 10.1 shows the payoff diagram.

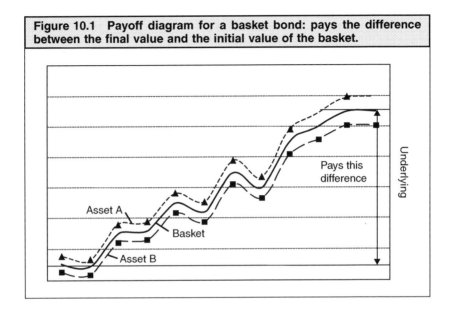

Figure 10.1 Payoff diagram for a basket bond: pays the difference between the final value and the initial value of the basket.

Risks

This structure is defined by a basic risk in the direction taken by the underlying, the interest rate, and the correlation, which will directly affect the volatility (Figures 10.2 and 10.3).

For the investor

Whoever buys this structure is determining some bullish expectations for the underlying assets which make up the basket. It is expected that relative growth in this basket will exceed the risk-free interest rate valid for the structure's term. These are accompanied by some bullish expectations in terms of the particular volatility in the underlying asset. In this sense the correlation that exists between the shares making up the basket will be the determining factor in its volatility and therefore in the option value. In general, the person buying the basket will enjoy increases in the correlation and volatility of the components, and consequently the basket.

For the issuer

The issuer has the opposite profile. If the issuer were not to take any hedging, he would run the risk of paying higher returns than the interbank deposit interest rates which apply at the moment of launch. Moreover, he would be

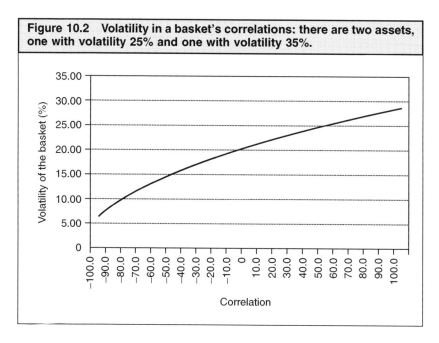

Figure 10.2 Volatility in a basket's correlations: there are two assets, one with volatility 25% and one with volatility 35%.

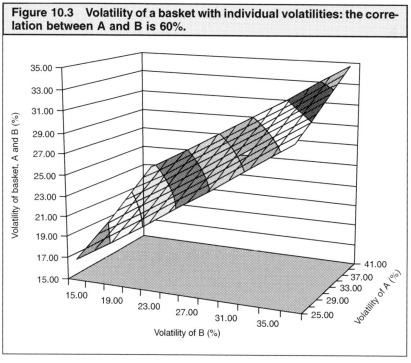

Figure 10.3 Volatility of a basket with individual volatilities: the correlation between A and B is 60%.

harmed by an increase in volatility of the underlying and its correlation, since his net position would be to sell the options (see later). Eventual short-term interest rate falls during the life of the structure would also assume a negative opportunity cost for him, in relation to the liability secured through the basket bond.

Construction

Construction begins with the issue of a zero coupon deposit and a share basket call option (which serves as a reference on the structure). The strike is established on the date when the operation is agreed. Where this offers a return, according to movement of the basket since the outset, this will be equal to how the basket is quoted on the market at the moment of launch. If, at maturity, the underlying, i.e. the basket, would have exceeded the strike, then the total interest that must be paid to the investor will be the appreciation between the strike and the final value of the basket.

A person that invests in a basket bond structure invests a principal, through which he will be paid just the interest derived from percentage growth in the basket until maturity. For this, the investor receives from the issuer a standard European option. For the issuer to guarantee 100% principal to the investor when the structure matures, the option handed to him will have a value limited by the difference between the principal and its present value, taking into consideration the market interest rate and term until maturity.

Example

Let's assume a structure where the customer is offered a one-year bond, on which will be paid the appreciation of a basket of two shares, A and B. Here are its values at the moment of issue.

	Share A	Share B
Price (€)	10	16
Dividend (%)	4	3
Volatility (%)	35	25

Both shares have the same weighting in the basket, which consists of the average value of the two titles, whose correlation is 60%. Let's assume, moreover, that a 37.9% rise in basket value is guaranteed. Here are the remaining data items:

- Interest rate: 4%
- Time: 1 year

Indicative terms

Description	Bond in euros with return linked to a basket comprising two shares, A and B
Nominal	€1 000 000
Issue price	100%
Interest	Variable according to growth in the basket during the operation term. Interest will be equal to 37.90% of its appreciation between start and maturity of operation
Term	1 year
Depreciation	100% nominal guaranteed

Valuation of this structure requires calculation of the basket's European call value with the following characteristics:

- Underlying: €13 (average of A and B)
- Weighting: 50% and 50%
- Strike: €13.00
- Time: 1 year
- Rate: 4%
- Dividend yield: 3.5% (average of A and B).
- Volatility of A: 35%
- Volatility of B: 25%
- Correlation: 60%

The volatility of the basket will be 25.85% (see later). So the option value from the Black–Scholes model will be

$$\text{Call} = e^{-qT}SN(d_1) - Ke^{-rT}N(d_2)$$
$$= 2.7182^{-3.5\%\times1} \times 13 \times N(0.14859) - 13 \times 2.7182^{-4\%\times1}$$
$$\times N(-0.10991) = 1.31926$$
$$d_1 = \frac{\ln(13/13) + [4\% - 3.5\% + \frac{1}{2}(25.851\%)^2] \times 1}{25.851\% \times \sqrt{1}} = 0.14859$$
$$d_2 = 0.14859 - 25.851\% \times \sqrt{1} = -0.10991$$

The option would cost 1.31926 index points, i.e. 10.14852% of the nominal, or €101 485:

$$1.31926/13 = 10.14852\%$$
$$10.14852\% \times 1\,000\,000 = €101\,485$$

To guarantee refund of the €1 000 000 within one year, its present value must be invested at the outset. This value is $1\,000\,000/(1 + 4\%) = €961\,538$, which leaves €38 462 available to purchase the option. Since the option value to cover the whole rise is €101 485, we can show that, where there is equilibrium, the issuer might only offer in effect a 37.9% appreciation of the basket:

$$38\,462/101\,485 = 37.90\%$$

Valuation

We need to calculate these two quantities:

- A call bond until the structure matures
- A standard European call option

We will obtain the call value using the Black–Scholes model for assets which pay dividends. The main difference will be the need to obtain a volatility that is unique to the basket, starting with individual volatilities and correlation coefficients between the components.

The volatility set of a basket of assets may be approximated analytically under the assumption that the basket price is lognormal (Sánchez and Tarriba 1999). If the basket price is given by

$$A = \sum_i w_i P_i$$

where P_i is the instrument price of the highest i and w_i is its weighting in the basket. The approximation consists of the assumption that $\ln A_T$ is distributed normally with mean μ and variance σ^2, in which case the moment-generating function for the normal distribution is

$$E(A_T^k) = \exp \tfrac{1}{2}(k\mu + k^2\sigma^2)$$

From which we obtain the first two moments:

$$\mu = 2 \ln E(A_T) - \tfrac{1}{2} \ln E(A_T^2) \tag{10.2}$$

$$\sigma^2 = \ln E(A_T^2) - 2 \ln E(A_T) \tag{10.3}$$

Here σ is the volatility of the basket, which will be the one used in the Black–Scholes model to valuate the basket options. The problem is reduced to calculating the expected value of the basket price and its square. It is assumed that each of the basket's components follows a lognormal distribution:

$$dP_i = P_i\mu_i \, dt + P_i\sigma_i \, dz_i$$

From which we can obtain the expected value for each of the components:

$$E(P_i) = P_{i0}e^{\mu T} = F_i$$

On the other hand, applying Itô's lemma, it can be shown that

$$E(P_i^2) = P_{i0}^2 e^{2\mu_i T} e^{2\sigma_i^2 T} = F_i^2 e^{\sigma_i^2 T}$$
$$E(P_i P_j) = P_i P_j e^{\mu_i T} e^{\mu_j T} e^{\rho_{ij}\sigma_i\sigma_j T}$$

This finally gives us that

$$E(A_T) = \sum_i w_i F_i$$

and

$$E(A_T^2) = \sum_i w_i^2 F_i^2 e^{\sigma_i^2 T} + 2\sum_{j>1} w_i w_j F_i F_j e^{\rho_{ij}\sigma_i\sigma_j T}$$

$$\sigma_{annual} = \sigma/\sqrt{T}$$

In our example the volatility was obtained using the following steps.

Step 1

The forward prices of the two shares are

$$P_{fA} = 10e^{(4\%-4\%)\times 1} = 10.00$$
$$P_{fB} = 16e^{(4\%-3\%)\times 1} = 16.16$$

Taking their average gives us the expected value $E(A_T) = 13.08$.

Step 2

Calculate the expected values for the square terms.

	$w_i^2 F_i^2 e^{\sigma_i^2 T}$
Share A	28.26
Share B	69.50

From which we obtain

$$\sum_i w_i^2 F_i^2 e^{\sigma_i^2 T} = 97.76$$

Step 3

Calculate the expected values for the cross terms:

$$w_A w_B F_A F_B e^{\rho_{AB}\sigma_A \sigma_B T} = 50\% \times 50\% \times 10.00 \times 16.16 e^{60\% \times 35\% \times 25\% \times 1}$$
$$= 42.58$$

For a basket of more than two assets, use

$$\sum w_i w_j F_i F_j e^{\rho_{ij}\sigma_i \sigma_j T}$$

Step 4

Find the value of $E(A_T^2)$:

$$E(A_T^2) = 97.76 + (2 \times 42.58) = 182.92$$

Step 5

Find the value of σ^2:

$$\sigma^2 = \ln 182.92 - 2 \ln 13.08$$
$$= 6.6827\%$$

and the volatility of the basket turns out to be

$$\sigma = 25.8509\%$$

The price of the structure at any moment is given by

Basket bond price = call(underlyings, strike, volatility, correlation,

rate, dividends, time) + present value of the principal

(100% or percentage of this guaranteed)

11

SPREAD BOND

Definition and commercial presentation

Spread bonds allow retail investors to finance their share purchases by the sale of another share or by simple speculation on the spread of two shares, without dealing directly with them. The final investor is offered an investment whose return is given by the movement of the spread between the two shares. In this way, the investor is implicitly taking a position on the spread using an investment where the return will depend directly on this spread.

The maturity is usually short to medium term. Depending on the case involved, the whole principal is guaranteed or only part of it, or alternatively, when the principal is guaranteed, then only a percentage is offered on the appreciation of the differential or spread of the two shares or indices. This is determined by the term and market position.

$$\text{Payoff} = \max(0, (S_{1T} - S_{2T})) \times \text{percent initial investment} \qquad (11.1)$$

where

K = price or initial reference spread
S_{1T} = price of underlying 1 at maturity T
S_{2T} = price of underlying 2 at maturity T

Figure 11.1 shows the payoff diagram.

Risks

This structure is defined by a basic risk in the direction taken by the underlying, interest rate, and correlation (Figure 11.2). The option involved is inversely

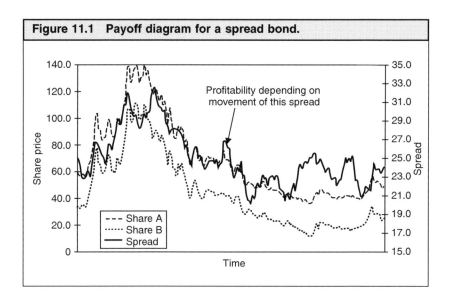

Figure 11.1   Payoff diagram for a spread bond.

Figure 11.2   Effect of correlation on a spread option: the volatilities are assumed to be equal for the two assets, at 25% for a one-year investment.

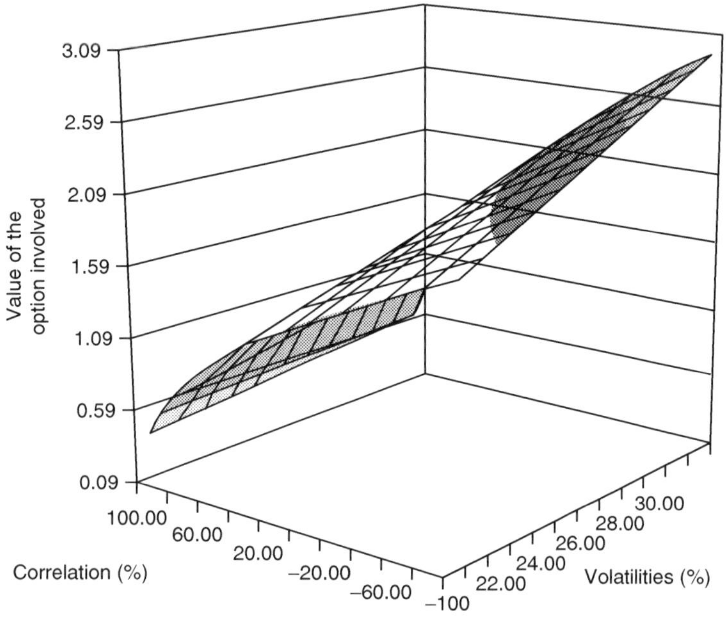

linked to the correlation. In a spread bond structure, the option involved will be for the investor, so the investor will have a negative sensitivity to the correlation, as we shall see later on. The extreme case is a 100% negative correlation; this implies that the spread will have a tendency to record movements (in both directions) if any of its components move. Thus, the probability of obtaining profits from an eventual movement, which might benefit any direction taken implicitly by the spread, will strengthen the option value and therefore the structure for the person who acquires it.

For the investor

Whoever buys this structure is determining some bullish expectations in price difference of the assets involved. It is expected that growth in this spread will exceed the risk-free interest rate for the structure's term. These are accompanied by some bullish expectations about the particular volatility of the underlying assets. The buyer will gain from a decrease in the correlation and an increase in the volatility of the implied assets.

For the issuer

If the issuer were not to take any hedging, he would run the risk of paying returns higher than interbank deposit interest rates at the moment of launch. Moreover, he would be harmed by an increase in volatility of the underlying and a decrease in the correlation, since he is the seller in this structure. Eventual reductions in short-term interest rates, during the life of the structure, would also assume he has a negative opportunity cost relative to the financing secured.

Construction

Construction begins with the issue of a zero coupon bond and a reference share call spread. The strike is established at the moment the structure is agreed; it is equal to how the spread is quoted in the market at that time. This is when a return is offered according to movement of the spread since the start. At maturity, the total interest payable to the investor will be given by the difference between the initial and final values of the spread, whenever this has moved in the right direction. In the opposite case, the investor will recover the principal without any additional return.

For the issuer to guarantee 100% of the principal to the investor when the structure matures, the option handed to him will have a value limited by the difference between the principal and its present value, taking into consideration the interest rate and term until maturity. If this difference were insufficient to deliver an option covering 100% of the appreciation, then the investor would only be offered the maximum percentage allowed. Put another way, if he were offered 100% of the spread gain, the principal guaranteed would be reduced at the end of the operation. This occurs if the option value exceeds the difference between the principal and its present value. Then the issuer might not invest sufficient capital today to have this capital at maturity, since he would have to buy this option to deliver it to the investor. What could be guaranteed would be the difference between the principal and the future option value. This would then cover 100% of the appreciation.

Example

Let's assume a structure where the investor is offered a one-year bond. On this he will be paid the increase in the difference, or spread, of two shares, A and B. The values are shown in the table, and the bond's correlation is 60% with 5% interest rate for one year.

	Share A	Share B
Price (€)	10	16
Dividend (%)	4	3
Volatility (%)	35	25

Indicative terms

Description	Bond in euros with profitability linked to movement of the spread $B - A$
Nominal	€1 000 000
Issue price	100%
Interest	Variable according to movement of the share spread during its term of operation. Interest will be equal to its variation between start and maturity of the operation
Term	1 year
Amortisation	100% nominal guaranteed

We will calculate what percentage of appreciation the investor might be offered. Valuation of this structure requires calculation of the spread call option value between the two shares with the following characteristics:

- Price A: €10
- Price B: €16

- Spread: €6
- Strike: €6
- Time: 1 year
- Rate: 5%
- Dividend A: 4%
- Dividend B: 3%
- σ of A: 35%
- σ of B: 25%
- Correlation: 60%

The option calculated by numerical integration would be worth 28.75%, that is $1\,000\,000 \times 28.7478\% = €287\,478$. To guarantee refund of the €1\,000\,000 within one year, its present value must be invested at the outset, namely $100\,000\,000/(1 + 5\%) = €952\,381$. This leaves €47\,619 available to buy the option. As the option giving 100% cover to the eventual rise in spread of the two shares is worth €287\,468, we will show that the issuer, in conditions of equilibrium, could only offer a 16.56% increase held by this spread:

$$47\,619/287\,478 = 16.56\%$$

Another possibility is not to offer any guarantee for the 100% principal in order to be able to offer 100% of the appreciation. Then the capital guaranteed would be

$$\frac{(1\,000\,000 - 287\,478) \times (1 + 5\%)}{1\,000\,000} = 74.81\%$$

The alternative is to lengthen the terms, which will make these structures more attractive in terms of guarantees or percentage appreciation, lowering the present value to guarantee the final principal. This increases the price of the option, but in proportion to the effect on the capital, the price increase will be lower.

Valuation

We will need to calculate these two quantities:

- A call bond until the structure matures
- Spread call option

Except in the special case of zero strike, an analytical equation cannot be obtained to valuate these options. If we assume the correlated underlyings are distributed according to a lognormal model, then generally speaking there is no analytical equation for the spread option value, and to obtain a solution we must turn to numerical integration techniques (Simpson,

Romberg, etc.):

$$w = e^{-r(T-t)} \int_0^\infty \int_0^\infty \max(w_1 x - w_2 y - K, 0) \, \mathrm{dDlnNB}(x, y) \, dx \, dy \quad (11.2)$$

$$w = e^{-r(T-t)} \int_{-\infty}^\infty \int_{-\infty}^\infty \max(w_1 x_0 - e^{\xi} - w_2 y_0 e^{\zeta} - K, 0) \mathrm{dDNB}(\xi, \zeta) \, d\xi \, d\zeta$$

$$(11.3)$$

where

$$\mathrm{dDNB}(u, v) = \frac{1}{2\pi \sigma_1 \sigma_2 \sqrt{1 - \rho^2}} \exp\left\{ \frac{1}{2(1 - \rho^2)} \left[-\left(\frac{u - \mu_1}{\sigma_1}\right)^2 \right.\right.$$

$$\left.\left. - 2\rho \left(\frac{u - \mu_1}{\sigma_1}\right) \left(\frac{v - \mu_2}{\sigma_2}\right) + \left(\frac{v - \mu_2}{\sigma_2}\right)^2 \right] \right\}$$

is the density function of the bivariate normal distribution with correlation ρ, and dDlnNB(x, y) is its equivalent lognormal distribution. ρ is the correlation coefficient between the returns of assets x and y.

An alternative way to carry out the valuation is to take the bivariate distribution and rearrange it to produce a univariate distribution (Zhang 1998, pp. 491–94; Vidal 2000). This will use density functions from a semianalytical equation for the option value:

$$w(x, y, t) = e^{-r(T-t)} \left(w_1 x e^{\mu_1(T-t)} A_1 - w_2 y e^{\mu_2(T-t)} A_2 - K A_3 \right) \quad (11.4)$$

where

$w_1 = 1$
$w_2 = 1$
x = price of instrument x
y = price of instrument y

and

$$A_1 = \int_{-\infty}^\infty f(u) N \left[\frac{d + \rho u + \sigma_1 \sqrt{T - t} + \Phi(u + \rho \sigma_1 \sqrt{T - t})}{\sqrt{1 - \rho^2}} \right] du$$

$$(11.5)$$

$$A_2 = \int_{-\infty}^\infty f(u) N \left[\frac{d + \rho u + \sigma_2 \sqrt{T - t} + \Phi(u + \sigma_2 \sqrt{T - t})}{\sqrt{1 - \rho^2}} \right] du \quad (11.6)$$

$$A_3 = \int_{-\infty}^\infty f(u) N \left[\frac{d + \rho u + \Phi(u)}{\sqrt{1 - \rho^2}} \right] du \quad (11.7)$$

$$d = d(w_1 x, K, \sigma_1, \mu_1, T - t) = \frac{1}{\sigma_1 \sqrt{T - t}}$$
$$\times \left[\ln \left(\frac{w_1 x}{K} \right) + \left(\mu_1 - \tfrac{1}{2}\sigma_1^2 \right) (T - t) \right] \tag{11.8}$$

$$\Phi(u) = -\frac{1}{\sigma \sqrt{T - t}} \ln \left\{ 1 + \frac{w_2 y}{K} \exp \left[\left(\mu_2 - \tfrac{1}{2}\sigma_2^2 \right) (T - t) + u\sigma_2 \sqrt{T - t} \right] \right\} \tag{11.9}$$

$$f(u) = \frac{1}{\sqrt{2\pi}} \exp \left(-\frac{u^2}{2} \right) \tag{11.10}$$

Equally, the parameters A_1, A_2 and A_3 must be calculated by numerical integration.

A further interesting technique for evaluating this type of option is based on a semianalytical approach to the payoff result, using standard European calls and puts. Linear approximations are carried out, subsequently, through consecutive tranches with these. This avoids numerical integration at the expense of valuating a relatively extensive plain vanilla option portfolio (Pearson 1995; Vidal 2000).

Having obtained the option value, we then need to determine the capital to be guaranteed. This is in relation to the percentage appreciation that may be offered to the investor. We will always start from the fundamental premise that to guarantee refund of this invested capital (capital$_0$) when the operation matures, then once the issuer receives the capital, he must invest the present value of this capital, at the outset, as if it were being paid back on maturity. The investment necessary to refund, at a future date, the same amount being invested today, is its present value. For this, we need to remember that, given an initial capital (capital$_0$) invested by the investor, if he wants to guarantee that on maturity capital$_T$ = capital$_0$ then the required investment is

$$\frac{\text{capital}_T}{(1 + r)^T}$$

where

capital$_T$ = the same capital at a future time T, i.e. at maturity
r = risk-free interest rate
T = time in years

We can also calculate capital − required investment = availability; this is the capital available to invest in options which the issuer will deliver in consideration to the investor. If the option value is greater than this difference, then there are two possibilities:

- Offer the investor a participation percentage in movement of the underlying, lower than the 100%, which would be

$$\frac{\text{availability}}{\text{option value}}$$

- Offer 100% participation in movement of the underlying, to avoid the need to guarantee 100% of the capital; the guarantee might be

$$\text{Percentage of guarantee} = \frac{(\text{capital}_0 - \text{option value}) \times (1 + r)^T}{\text{capital}_0}$$

In our example, to offer 100% appreciation of the best two shares, it would only be possible to guarantee that, at the end, there would be a refund of 74.81% of the capital invested. The interests, in this case, would collect 100% of the appreciation (if it existed) of the best two movements in the shares.

The structure price at any moment will be given by

Spread bond price = call[underlyings(A, B), strikes(A, B) volatilities(A, B),

correlation, rates(A, B), dividends(A, B), time]

+ present value of the principal (100% or

percentage of this guaranteed)

12

BEST-OF BOND

Definition and commercial presentation

There are many terms and conditions for best-of bonds. The most usual in equity derivatives are those where the investor profits from the most suitable individual movement of a set of stock market assets. This concerns a structure whose yield is the best performance by the assets in the set of chosen assets. Even if a basket is formed, the profitability of the structure is not given by its total movement. In fact, it is possible to imagine a case where the real value of the basket would record a fall but the structure would generate a positive return for the investor.

The investor in a best-of bond will receive interest through his investment, which in percentage terms will be equal to the appreciation of the best asset or reference index determined on a fixed date in relation to the outset.

Maturity is usually medium to long term. Depending on the case involved, the whole principal is guaranteed or only part of it; or alternatively, when the principal is guaranteed, only a percentage of the appreciation of the best of the assets involved is offered. This is determined by the term and market position.

$$\text{Payoff} = \max\left[0, \frac{(S_{1T} - K_1)}{K_1}, \frac{(S_{2T} - K_2)}{K_2}\right]$$
$$\times \text{ percent initial investment } (\leq 100\%) \quad (12.1)$$

where

S = underlying
K = reference price for the appreciation
T = time to maturity

Figure 12.1 shows the payoff diagram.

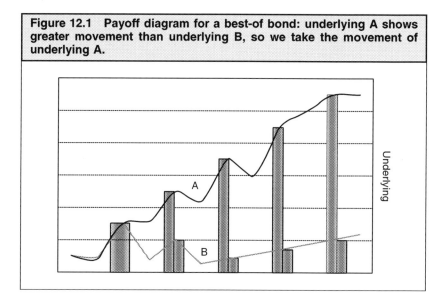

Figure 12.1 Payoff diagram for a best-of bond: underlying A shows greater movement than underlying B, so we take the movement of underlying A.

Risks

This structure is defined by a fundamental risk in the direction taken by the underlyings, interest rate, and correlation, although in best-of structures the option involved will appear to be linked inversely to the correlation between the assets (Figure 12.2). Considering that in a best-of structure the option involved is for the investor, the investor will have a negative sensitivity to the correlation, as we shall see later on.

For the investor

Whoever buys this structure is determining some bullish expectations of the underlying assets, which make up the basket from which the best will be chosen, or at least, some bullish expectations of some of them. It is expected that the relative growth of some will exceed the risk-free interest rate valid for the structure. These are accompanied by some bullish expectations in terms of the particular volatility of the underlying assets. In general, the buyer will benefit from reductions in the correlation and rises in volatility of the components.

For the issuer

The issuer has the opposite profile. Were he not to take out cover, he would run the risk of paying returns higher than interbank deposit interest rates valid

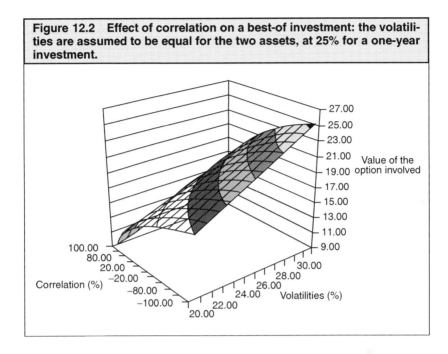

Figure 12.2   Effect of correlation on a best-of investment: the volatilities are assumed to be equal for the two assets, at 25% for a one-year investment.

at the moment of launch. Moreover, he would be harmed by an increase in volatility of the underlyings and the decrease of his correlation. This is because he is in the position of seller. Eventual reductions in short-term interest rates during the life of the structure would also assume he has a negative opportunity cost relative to the finance secured through the best-of bond shares.

Construction

Construction begins with the issue of a zero coupon bond and a best-of call option with a share variation percentage. The shares are established as reference in the structure. On the date the operation is agreed, the strikes are established, and where they offer a return that depends on the movement in the best shares since the start, these strikes will be equal to how they are quoted at this initial moment. At maturity, the total interest to be paid to the investor will be the appreciation between the strike and the final share value, determined since the start by the greater percentage appreciation.

Anyone who invests in a best-of bond structure invests a principal, for which he will only be paid the interest derived from the best percentage growth in the share basket until maturity. For this, he receives from the issuer an at-the-money best-of call with respect to the spot. So the issuer can guarantee the investor 100% principal when the structure matures, the option handed to him will have a value limited by the difference between the principal and its present value, taking into consideration market interest rate and term until maturity. Consequently, if this difference is insufficient to deliver an option covering 100% of the appreciation, the investor will only be offered the maximum percentage taken on.

Alternatively, he might be offered 100% of the appreciation of the best shares, but then he might not be guaranteed 100% of the principal at maturity. This occurs if the option value exceeds the difference between the principal and its present value, and then the issuer might not invest enough money today to repay the principal at maturity. This is because he has to buy this option to deliver it to the investor. He could, however, guarantee the difference between the principal and the future option value. This would then cover 100% of the appreciation.

Example

Let's assume a structure where the customer is offered a one-year bond, on which he will be paid the best appreciation from a basket made up of shares A and B. The values are shown in the table, and the bond's correlation is 60% with 5% interest rate for one year.

	Share A	Share B
Price (€)	10	16
Dividend (%)	4	3
Volatility (%)	35	25

Indicative terms

Description	Bond in euros with profitability linked to the best percentage movement of two shares from a basket made up of A and B
Nominal	€1 000 000
Issue price	100%
Interest	Variable according to movement in the best shares during the operation term. Interest will be equal to its appreciation between the start and maturity of the operation
Term	1 year
Amortisation	100% nominal guaranteed

We will calculate what percentage of the appreciation could be offered to the investor. Valuation of this structure requires calculation of a best-of call option value from the percentage of two shares with the following characteristics:

- Price A: €10
- Price B: €16
- Strike A: €10
- Strike B: €16
- Time: 1 year
- Rate: 5%
- Dividend A: 4%
- Dividend B: 3%
- σ of A: 35%
- σ of B: 25%
- Correlation: 60%

Numerical integration indicates the option would be worth 18.27%, that is $1\,000\,000 \times 18.2669\% = €182\,669$. To guarantee refund of the €1 000 000 within one year, its present value must be invested at the outset, namely $100\,000\,000/(1 + 5\%) = €952\,381$. This leaves €47 619 available to buy the option. Since the option covering the whole rise in the best two shares is worth €182 669, we will show that, in conditions of equilibrium, the issuer might effectively only offer an appreciation of 26.07%:

$$47\,619/182\,669 = 26.07\%$$

Another possibility is not to offer any guarantee for the 100% principal in order to be able to offer 100% of the appreciation. Then the capital guaranteed would be

$$\frac{(1\,000\,000 - 182\,669) \times (1 + 5\%)}{1\,000\,000} = 85.85\%$$

To make these structures more attractive in terms of guarantees or percentage appreciation, the alternative is to lengthen the terms, lowering the present value to guarantee the final principal. This increases the price of the option, but in proportion to the effect on the capital, the price increase will be lower.

Valuation

We need to calculate these two quantities:

- A zero coupon bond until the structure matures
- Percentage best-of call option: to valuate this double-strike option, we may turn to numerical integration techniques such as the methods of Romberg and Simpson (Gerald and Wheatley 1999, pp. 377–85)

We must also approximate the continuous density function for the standard bivariate normal distribution:

$$\text{Call} = e^{-rT} \int_{-\infty}^{\infty} \int_{-\infty}^{\infty} \max\left[0, \frac{(S_{1T} - K_1)}{K_1}, \frac{(S_{2T} - K_2)}{K_2}\right] f(a, b)\, da\, db$$

where

S_{10} = price of underlying 1 at the present moment
S_{1T} = price of underlying 1 at maturity
S_{20} = price of underlying 2 at the present moment
S_{2T} = price of underlying 2 at maturity
r = risk-free interest rate
T = time in years
a = $\ln(S_{1T}/S_{10})$
b = $\ln(S_{2T}/S_{20})$

The relevant variables for the integration will be the prices of the two assets, their volatilities, their dividend returns and the correlation between them. Here is the model we will follow:

$$\text{Asset } a = (\text{forward price})_a \exp(-\tfrac{1}{2}\sigma_a^2 T + \sigma_a \sqrt{T}\varepsilon_a)$$

$$\text{Asset } b = (\text{forward price})_b \exp(-\tfrac{1}{2}\sigma_b^2 T + \sigma_b \sqrt{T}\varepsilon_b)$$

$$\text{Bivariate density function} = \frac{1}{2\pi\sqrt{1 - \rho^2}} \exp\left(-\frac{a^2 + b^2 - 2\rho ab}{2\sqrt{1 - \rho^2}}\right)$$

where

σ = volatility
ρ = correlation coefficient
T = time in years
ε = random variable

Having obtained the option value, we then need to determine the capital to be guaranteed. This is in relation to the percentage appreciation that may be offered to the investor. We will always start from the fundamental premise that to guarantee refund of this invested capital (capital$_0$) when the operation matures, then once the issuer receives the capital, he must invest the present value of this capital, at the outset, as if it were being paid back on maturity. The investment necessary to refund, at a future date, the same amount being invested today, is its present value. For this, we need to remember that, given an initial capital (capital$_0$) invested by the investor, if he wants to guarantee that on maturity capital$_T$ = capital$_0$ then the required investment is

$$\frac{\text{capital}_T}{(1+r)^T}$$

where

capital$_T$ = the same capital at a future time T, i.e. at maturity
r = risk-free interest rate
T = time in years

We can also calculate capital − required investment = availability; this is the capital available to invest in options which the issuer will deliver in consideration to the investor. If the option value is greater than this difference, then there are two possibilities:

- Offer the investor a participation percentage in movement of the underlying, lower than the 100%, which would be

$$\frac{\text{availability}}{\text{option value}}$$

- Offer 100% participation in movement of the underlying, to avoid the need to guarantee 100% of the capital; the guarantee might be

$$\text{Percentage of guarantee} = \frac{(\text{capital}_0 - \text{option value}) \times (1+r)^T}{\text{capital}_0}$$

In our example, to offer 100% of the appreciation of the best two shares, it might only be possible to guarantee that, at the end, there would be a refund of 85.85% of the capital invested. The interests, in this case, would collect 100% of the appreciation (if it existed) from the best two share movements.

The structure price at any moment will be given by

Best-of bond price = call[underlyings(a, b), strikes(a, b), volatilities(a, b),

correlation, rates(a, b), dividends(a, b), time]

+ present value of the principal (100% or

percentage of this guaranteed)

PART III

FIXED INCOME STRUCTURES

13

FLOATING RATE NOTE

Definition and commercial presentation

Floating rate notes are medium- and long-term titles with regular floating rate coupons linked to movement in an interest rate representative of the money market. Consequently, the risk assumed, relative to a floating rate note (FRN), is only attributable to the coupon already fixed. Nevertheless, in relation to what originally would have been a fixed rate of investment, the person buying an FRN assumes a risk of reductions in interest throughout the duration.

Maturity is usually medium and long term, based on 5 year and 20 year terms. Usually the issue goes out at par, the principal is guaranteed and a regular coupon is offered, linked to a reference index plus a spread according to the issuer's credit rating and market conditions.

$$\text{Payoff} = \text{coupons } f(\text{money market index}) + \text{principal}$$

Figure 13.1 shows the payoff diagram.

Risks

When dealing with floating coupon structures, there is no interest rate risk in absolute terms for those flows fixed at a future date. The issuer will be able to adapt financing of these flows to the same rates of market interest. From the investor's viewpoint, the absence of any interest rate risks is justified in absolute terms by the fact that financing of the capital necessary to buy the title may be adapted to the same market interests

Figure 13.1   Payoff diagram for a floating rate note: the floating flows are unknown until fixed; the column heights indicate the short-term interest rates.

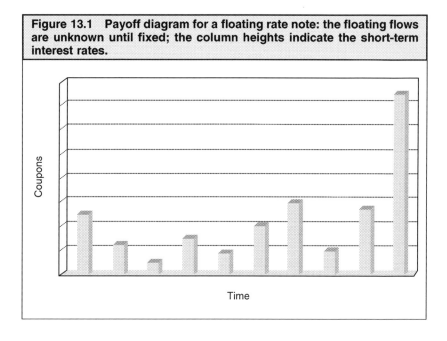

which serve as reference in the FRN. Compared with a fixed rate investment, at the outset of an FRN investment, the investor clearly runs the risk of interest rate reductions during the life of the title, and this creates an opportunity cost.

In any case, assuming there will always be at least a fixed interest, the FRN will hold a risk. In this way, the only relevant item will be duration of the first cash flow, namely duration of a zero coupon asset whose duration is the time between now and the payment date. When dealing with just one cash flow, the weighting factor for the remainder of its life is 100%, for which the duration will be the remaining life of this flow at the current moment.

Construction

The issuer of an FRN synthetically issues a fixed rate bond and sells an interest rate swap (IRS) to the investor. Through this, he collects the fixed rate and pays the short-term floating rate (Libor, Euribor, etc.). Specifically, the issuer must carry out these operations:

• Issue the fixed rate bond with coupon according to market conditions (according to price) and his credit rating.

- Sell an IRS: the issuer pays the short-term floating rate and receives the fixed rate. These flows must have the same frequency as undertaken for the bond offered to the investor.

Example

There is a 3 year FRN from an issuer (who, according to his credit rating at market conditions, would pay a fixed rate of 6% as opposed to a standard interbank risk of 5.41%), who offers 57bp (basis points) over 6 month Euribor floating rate spread, payable semiannually. Let's assume this is issued at par through a unit nominal of €10 million.

Indicative terms

Description	Bond in euros with floating coupons linked to a 6 month Euribor payable six-monthly
Nominal	€10 000 000
Issue price	100%
Interest	6 month Euribor + 57bp; basis Act/360
Term	3 years
Amortisation	100%

The structure consists in issuing a 3 year, 6% issuer fixed rate bond, which is 'swapped' with the investor through an IRS on which he will receive 6% and pay the 6 month Euribor. If we assume that the market IRS will be quoting 5.41%, then the floating that is payable will be Euribor + 57bp. This is obtained in the following way. Remember the value of a sold IRS is

$$\sum_{i=1}^{n} r_{\text{fixed}} \text{YF}_i \times \text{DF}_i \times \text{notional} - \sum_{i=1}^{m} r_{\text{imp}_i} \text{YF}_i \times \text{DF}_i \times \text{notional} \qquad (13.1)$$

This equation finds the difference between the present value of the future flows in the fixed branch and the present value of the future flows in the floating branch. This is estimated starting from the implicit rates. We can simplify this equation as follows:

present value of fixed branch − present value of floating branch

where

r_{fixed} = fixed interest rate
r_{imp} = implicit or forward interest rate

Table 13.1			
Term	Actual days	Par rate	Discount factor
O/N	3	5.00	0.9995835
T/N	5	4.35	0.9993420
1 day	6	4.35	0.9992213
1 week	12	4.38	0.9984916
1 month	38	4.46	0.9952730
2 months	67	4.54	0.9915889
3 months	97	4.46	0.9880801
4 months	129	4.57	0.9838623
5 months	158	4.67	0.9799118
6 months	189	4.77	0.9755579
7 months	220	4.82	0.9713898
8 months	248	4.86	0.9675886
9 months	279	4.91	0.9633414
10 months	311	4.96	0.9589477
11 months	340	5.00	0.9549363
1 year	370	5.04	0.9507583
2 years	735	5.32	0.9008371
3 years	1102	5.42	0.8526506
4 years	1466	5.49	0.8065834

Note: the rates of terms higher than 1 year correspond to an IRS whose fixed rate
is paid annually against a six-monthly floating.

YF = fraction of year in which it is accrued
DF = discount factor
n = number of fixed flows
m = number of variable flows

Given the two interest rates i_a and i_b from the deposits involved, we get

$$r_{\text{imp}} = \left(\frac{1 + r_b d_b / 36\,000}{1 + r_a d_a / 36\,000} - 1 \right) \frac{36\,000}{d_b - d_a} \qquad (13.2)$$

where

r_a = interest rate of deposit a (shortest period of those involved)
r_b = interest rate of deposit b (longest period of those involved)
d_a = days of life of deposit a (shortest period of those involved)
d_b = days of life of deposit b (longest period of those involved)

Table 13.1 shows the curve of the interest rate. Table 13.2 gives the IRS value
in our example. So we obtain

$$1\,623\,900 - 1\,465\,006 = €158\,894$$

Table 13.2

Years	Factor	Initial rate (%)	Flow	Present value
SIX-MONTHLY STANDARD FLOATING BRANCH				
0.51	0.97612	4.77	245 125	239 271
0.51	0.95118	5.19	262 238	249 434
0.51	0.92594	5.39	272 537	252 353
0.51	0.90137	5.39	272 587	245 702
0.51	0.87714	5.47	276 293	242 347
0.51	0.85355	5.47	276 376	235 900
			Total	1 465 006
ANNUAL FIXED BRANCH				
1.01	0.95118	6.00	603 333	573 876
1.00	0.90137	6.00	598 333	539 320
1.00	0.85355	6.00	598 333	510 704
			Total	1 623 900

Note: the interests of the floating and fixed branches are calculated according to the IRS standards in euros, respectively Act/360 and 30/360.

This means that the present value in the fixed branch exceeds the present value in the floating branch by €158 894. Through this, the person paying for the fixed branch will only be prepared to acquire the undertaking to pay the fixed rate on the operation if, in exchange, he receives the floating rate plus a spread whose present value must be €158 894. The spread will therefore be

$$(\text{IRS value}) \bigg/ \sum_{i=1}^{m} \text{YF}_i \times \text{DF}_i \times \text{notional} \qquad (13.3)$$

In our example the spread is

$$\frac{158\,894}{27\,812\,500} = 0.57\%$$

Table 13.3 gives the present value in euros of six flows payable every six months over a 3 year period and corresponding to 0.57%. In short, this FRN, if issued at a price of 100%, should offer interest equal to 6 month Euribor + 57bp.

Valuation

Valuation of an FRN will be reduced to calculating the present values of the floating flows with any corresponding spread:

Table 13.3 Present value spread (€).	
	−28 658
	−27 472
	−26 744
	−26 034
	−25 334
	−24 653
Total	−158 653

$$\text{Price} = (\text{principal} \times DF_{\text{maturity}}) + (r_f + \text{spread})YF_i \times DF_i \times \text{notional}$$

$$+ \sum_{i=1}^{m} (r_{\text{imp}_i} + \text{spread})YF_i \times DF_i \times \text{notional}$$

where

DF = discount factor
YF = fraction of year in which it is accrued
r_f = fixed interest rate (the first of the floating)
r_{imp} = implicit or forward interest rate

14

REVERSE FLOATING RATE NOTE

Definition and commercial presentation

Reverse floating rate notes are medium- and long-term titles with regular floating rate coupons linked to movement in an interest rate representative of the money market. The special feature is that floating coupons or variables in this structure will increase with respect to falls in the reference index, and fall with respect to increases in market interest rates represented by this index. We are dealing here with an FRN in which the investor must have some bearish expectations for interest rates that favour an increase in the coupons paid through this structure.

Usually they have medium- and long-term maturity from 5 to 20 years and they are issued at par, guaranteeing the principal and offering a regular coupon linked inversely to the reference index plus a spread, according to the issuer's credit rating.

$$\text{Payoff} = \text{coupons } f(T_x - \text{money market index}) \geq 0 + \text{principal}$$

where T_x is an interest rate that is n times the money market index. Figure 14.1 shows the payoff diagram.

Risks

A reverse FRN has the opposite risk profile of a standard FRN. Coupons collected by the investor move in the opposite way to reference interest rates.

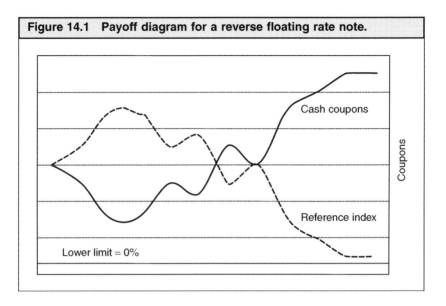

Figure 14.1 Payoff diagram for a reverse floating rate note.

This means we can no longer limit the risk analysis to comparing alternative fixed rate investments or to the suitability of financing the capital needed to buy the title at the appropriate reference rates. Compared to a fixed rate investment, it may well be certain that in a reverse FRN there is a risk for the investor that interest rates may rise during the life of the title, and this may create an opportunity cost. It is no less certain, however, that in a fixed rate investment, a rise in interest rates would have an opposite, double impact. Where a parallel rise occurs in the whole interest rate curve, it would favour reinvestment of the fixed coupons, which are collected at a fixed rate in fixed income assets. Nevertheless, the effect on the title's market price would be negative. Remember that the price of a fixed income asset is given by revaluation of its coupons. If the rates with which we are revaluing the coupons have suffered an increase, the price will evidently be lower, affecting the investment in a negative way.

Hypothetically, the risk of a reverse FRN for an investor is given by rises in the reference index. However, according to these rate rises, it may only be the buckets that affect this index (movement in the curve slope); or perhaps the level of risk relative to this investment, in respect of an alternative in a fixed coupon bond, will yield distinct results.

Construction

From a hypothetical viewpoint, the investor in a reverse FRN holds a purchased FRN and a sold fixed rate bond. On top of the standard FRN structure, we may add two derivative instruments: one that allows the flotation to head in the reverse direction, and another that prevents an investor from meeting negative interest. This is where the reference index rises significantly. The issuer of a reverse FRN must carry out these operations:

- Issue the fixed rate bond with coupon corresponding to market conditions (price driven) and his credit rating.
- Sell an IRS: the issuer pays the floating rate and collects the fixed rate. These flows must have the same frequency as undertaken on the bond offered to the investor.
- Purchase n IRS: this number will be given by the multiplier of market rate, determined by the minuend in coupon reference index.
- Sell a cap with strike $n \times$ fixed rate at par of the IRS.

The first two steps make up the IRS; the third step allows the flotation sign to be converted; and the final step prevents the investor from collecting negative interest.

Example

A 3 year reverse FRN from an issuer (depending on his credit rating, he would pay 5.34%, Act/360 per annum, with standard interbank risk), who offers a coupon at 10.68% (12 month Euribor), payable annually. Let's assume it is issued at par through a unit nominal of €10 million.

Indicative terms

Description	Bond in euros with floating coupons linked inversely to 12 month Euribor, payable annually. Coupon rate will be 10.68% − 12 month Euribor (Act/360) − 0.01% × value of the cap
Nominal	€10 000 000
Issue price	100%
Interest	10.68% − 12 month Euribor (Act/360) − 0.01% value of the cap
Term	3 years
Amortisation	100%

Just as fixing of interest is determined, we could say, at least theoretically, that the investor receives in this structure a fixed coupon and 'pays' the market floating. Certainly the investor will never pay for an interest, because the structure has built into it a derivative which avoids this, known as a cap. But the coupon, defined as the difference between a fixed rate and the reference index, might be understood to be just this, from a theoretical and financial point of view. Starting from this premise, both its hedge and valuation would be carried out simply by a fixed number of IRS purchased by the issuer. This number will be given by the multiplier of market rate, determined by the minuend in coupon reference index.

Using the data of Table 13.1, we quote the IRS rates for greater than or equal to 2 years; according to convention, we quote them in euros with a six-month frequency in the floating branch (Act/360) and an annual frequency in the fixed branch (30/360). If we level out the frequency rate to once per year, with basis Act/360, the 3 year rate would be 5.34% instead of the 5.42% shown in Table 13.1. The fixed coupon is double this. We need to perform a valuation of two IRS in the market.

The investor receives

Fixed coupon F (double the market) − floating rate V

≈ received fixed rate (double the market in this example)

and pays floating

The issuer pays

Fixed coupon (double the market) − floating rate

≈ fixed payment (double the market in this example)

and receives floating

We will show that, collecting on two IRS in the market at 5.34% and paying the floating in the same ratio, the issuer would rely on the flows necessary to pay the investor the interest, determined in the contract, on each date the interest falls due. Table 14.1 shows the flows in each of the IRS for which the issuer should sign a contract with a third party. Bear in mind that the investor implicitly pays for the Euribor (in reality this is deducted from the 10.68%), through which, with this hedge, the issuer would have a net cost equal to the Euribor. In fact, he receives through the IRS the total of the two fixed flows and the two floating flows, but collects from the investor a floating that amounts to a 12 month Euribor floating net cost.

Where in this structure the 12 month Euribor would exceed 10.68%, there would be an anomalous position of negative interest payment to the investor. To avoid this, the investor receives from the issuer a cap with the aforementioned strike. In our example the investor receives a 3 year cap with strike at 10.68% with implicit FRA call options with annual maturity. With implied market volatility of 18%, the value of this cap would be €1753 (0.02% over the nominal or 0.01% in a 3 year spread) for a nominal of €10 000 000.

Table 14.1

Date	Days	Interdays	Year fraction	Factor	Implied (%)	Flow	Present value of flow
			VARIABLE				
Today							
1 year	365	365	1.0139	0.9515	5.04	511 000	486 193
2 years	730	365	1.0139	0.9015	5.46	554 079	499 504
3 years	1095	365	1.0139	0.8535	5.54	561 866	479 578
			FIXED				
Today							
1 year	365	365	1.0139	0.9515	5.34	541 391	515 108
2 years	730	365	1.0139	0.9015	5.34	541 391	488 065
3 years	1095	365	1.0139	0.8535	5.34	541 391	462 101

From there, the 0.01% is left over as total profit in the structure, by way of the cap given to the investor.

Valuation

To find the price of a reverse FRN, we must perform a valuation of the IRS involved. The number of IRS will be given by the multiplier of market rate, determined by the reduction in coupon reference index. Likewise, the cap must be valuated. The cap's strike coincides with this rate and will always be for the investor. In this sense, remember that the value of a cap is given by the total of each of the implicit rate call options it comprises; these are known as caplets (Hull 2000). Once it has been issued, the value of a reverse FRN will be given by the corresponding number n of IRS, whose fixed rate will have been given, since at the moment of issue it was in force at the prevailing market conditions:

$$\text{Cap} = \sum_{i=1}^{n} \text{caplets}[\text{underlying}(r_{\text{imp}_i}), \text{strike, time}, r_i, \text{volatility}] \qquad (14.1)$$

and each caplet will be

$$\tau \times \text{notional} \times e^{-r(k+1)\tau}[F_k N(d_1) - KN(d_2)] \qquad (14.2)$$

$$d_1 = \frac{\ln(F_k/K) + \sigma^2 k\tau/2}{\sigma\sqrt{k\tau}}$$

$$d_2 = \frac{\ln(F_k/K) - \sigma^2 k\tau/2}{\sigma\sqrt{k\tau}} = d_1 - \sigma\sqrt{k\tau}$$

where

τ = fraction of year of accrual of underlying interest
r = risk-free interest rate
$k\tau$ = moment of fixing the rate for settlement of the option
$(k+1)\tau$ = moment of option's settlement
F_k = implicit or forward rate at moment k
K = strike

$$\text{Price} = (\text{principal} \times \text{DF}_{\text{maturity}}) + (r_f + \text{spread}) \times \text{YF}_i \times \text{DF}_i \times \text{notional}$$

$$+ \sum_{i=1}^{m} (r_{\text{fixed}} - r_{\text{imp}_i}) + \text{spread} \times \text{YF}_i \times \text{DF}_i \times \text{notional}$$

$$+ \text{cap}[\text{underlying}(r_{\text{imp}_i}), \text{strike}(r_{\text{fixed}}), \text{time}, r_i, \text{volatility}]$$

where

DF = discount factor
YF = fraction of year of accrual
r_f = fixed interest rate (the first of the floating)
r_{imp} = implicit or forward interest rate
r_{fixed} = fixed interest rate

r_{fixed} appears as a reducing term in the equation which determines the coupon in the reverse FRN structure.

This price equation presents the relevant symbols from the viewpoint of the investor, who is considering the positive future flows in the reverse FRN. This is just like in the implicit position purchased in the cap with strike n times the rate like swap at the moment of issue. This allows him to be assured of a minimum profitability, which is not binding but is never negative.

15

COLLARED FLOATING RATE NOTE

Definition and commercial presentation

Collared floating rate notes are floating rate medium- and long-term titles with periodic coupons linked to an interest rate representative of the money market. A floor in the interest is established, although a maximum return is also established at the time. Here we are dealing with an FRN in which the investor renounces potential rises in rates above a determined level, with the aim of also having limits to eventual reductions in the reference index for the interest payment.

Usually they have a medium- and long-term maturity from 5 to 20 years, and are issued at par, guaranteeing the principal and offering a regular coupon linked to the reference index plus a spread, depending on the issuer's credit rating and market conditions. All this is submitted to a limited range in fluctuation.

$$\text{Payoff} = \text{coupons } f(\text{floor} < \text{money market index} < \text{cap}) + \text{principal}$$

Figure 15.1 shows the payoff diagram.

Risks

For the investor, a collared FRN has risks similar to those of a standard FRN, but now they are limited upwards and downwards financed *floor* by a *cap*. In short, the investor counteracts eventual reductions in reference index interest

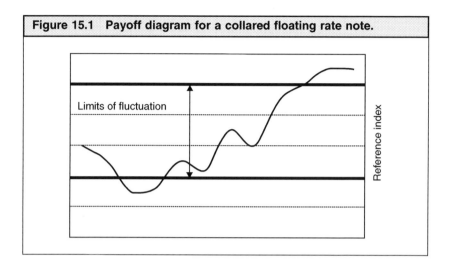

Figure 15.1   Payoff diagram for a collared floating rate note.

rates at the expense of giving up eventual rises in this index above another level. The floating nature of the investment is restricted to a determined range.

Construction

A collared FRN is constructed like a standard FRN but the collared structure allows the index movements to be limited. This is relevant for fixing the coupons. The issuer of a collared FRN must carry out these operations synthetically:

- Issue the fixed rate bond with coupon corresponding to the market conditions (price driven) and his credit rating.
- Sell an IRS: the issuer pays the floating rate and collects on the fixed rate. These flows must have the same frequency as for the bond offered to the investor.
- Sell a floor with strike at the interest rate level, on which a limit is set on the reference index downward fall, in order to fix the coupons.
- Purchase a cap with strike at the interest rate level, on which a limit is set on the reference index upward rise, in order to fix the coupons.

If the cap value equals the floor value, the investor will not see any rebound in the existence of the collar, or the range of fluctuation limits in the reference index; this is with respect to a standard FRN. In the opposite case, what must be assumed is the part cost of the 'downward hedge' in the reference index. This receives a floating interest, lower by any measure, as we shall now see.

Example

There is a 3 year FRN from an issuer (who would pay a fixed rate of 6%, as opposed to the standard interbank risk of 5.41%, depending on his credit rating) who offers 57bp over 6 month Euribor spread, payable every six months. Let's assume this is issued at par through a unit nominal of €10 million and let's assume the investor is guaranteed a maximum range of fluctuation in 6 month Euribor between 6% and 5.05% without any additional cost.

Indicative terms

Description	Bond in euros with floating coupons linked to 6 month Euribor, payable every six months. Its fluctuation is limited to the range 5.05% to 6%
Nominal	€10 000 000
Issue price	100%
Interest	6 month Euribor + 57bp; basis Act/360
Term	3 years
Amortisation	100%

This example is based on the example in Chapter 13, so we may investigate it by modifying our results for the standard FRN. For this, valuation will be carried out on a zero cost collar, which the investor receives on the structure. The person holding a collar is long in a cap and a sold floor. In the case of a zero cost collar, both have the same value.

Table 13.1 gives the interest rate curve. In our example the investor receives a 3 year floor with strike at 5.05%, with options (implicit FRA put maturing every 6 months). With an implied market volatility of 15.30%, the value of this floor would be €53 303 (0.53% over nominal or 0.23% on a 3 year spread) for a nominal of €10 000 000.

The investor grants the issuer a cap with strike at 6%, which in this example completely finances the floor value. This means it also has a value of €53 303 (0.53% over nominal or 0.23% on a 3 year spread) taking into consideration an implied volatility of 17.60%.

If we consider that value of the floor − value of the cap = 0, then the value of the FRN will continue to be the same, although a limit will be set in terms of fluctuation of the reference index between 5.05% and 6%, and therefore a choice of possible values for the FRN coupons, between 5.62% (5.05% + 0.57%) and 6.57% (6% + 0.57%).

Valuation

Besides calculating the present values in the variable flows with any corresponding spread, valuation of a collared FRN requires us to analyse the collar. In this sense, remember that the value of a cap is given by the total of each of the implicit rate call options it comprises; these are known as caplets (Hull 2000):

$$\text{Cap} = \sum_{i=1}^{n} \text{caplets}(r_{\text{imp}_i}, K_i, T_i, r_i, \sigma_i) \tag{15.1}$$

where

r_{imp_i} = implied rate of underlying
K = strike
T_i = time to expiry
σ_i = implied volatility
r_i = risk-free interest rate

Each caplet will be

$$\tau \times \text{notional} \times e^{-r(k+1)\tau}[F_k N(d_1) - KN(d_2)] \tag{15.2}$$

and each floorlet will be

$$\tau \times \text{notional} \times e^{-r(k+1)\tau}[-F_k N(d_1) + KN(d_2)] \tag{15.3}$$

with

$$d_1 = \frac{\ln(F_k/K) + \sigma^2 k\tau/2}{\sigma\sqrt{k\tau}}$$

$$d_2 = \frac{\ln(F_k/K) - \sigma^2 k\tau/2}{\sigma\sqrt{k\tau}} = d_1 - \sigma\sqrt{k\tau}$$

where

τ = fraction of year of accrual of underlying interest
r = risk-free interest rate
$k\tau$ = moment of fixing the rate for settlement of the option
$(k+1)\tau$ = moment of option's settlement
F_k = implicit or forward rate at moment k
K = strike

$$\text{Price} = (\text{principal} \times \text{DF}_{\text{maturity}}) + (r_f + \text{spread}) \times \text{YF}_i \times \text{DF}_i \times \text{notional}$$

$$+ \sum_{i=1}^{m} (r_{\text{fixed}} - r_{\text{imp}_i}) + \text{spread} \times \text{YF}_i \times \text{DF}_i \times \text{notional}$$

$$+ \text{floor}[\text{underlying}(r_{\text{imp}_i}), \text{strike}, \text{time}, r_i, \text{volatility}]$$

$$- \text{cap}[\text{underlying}(r_{\text{imp}_i}), \text{strike}, \text{time}, r_i, \text{volatility}]$$

where

DF = discount factor
YF = fraction of year of accrual
r_f = fixed interest rate (the first of the floating)
r_{imp} = implicit or forward interest rate
r_{fixed} = fixed interest rate

This price equation presents relevant signs from the viewpoint of the investor, when considering the positive future flows in the FRN, just like the implicit position of the floor purchased and the cap sold. This allows him to have minimum assured profitability through coupons, at the expense of another rising limit within these.

16

DIGITAL RANGES
(CORRIDOR
NOTES)

Definition and commercial presentation

The digital ranges covered in Chapter 7 will now be analysed in structures linked to interbank reference interest rates such as Euribor or Libor. The philosophy is the same as for ranges linked to stock price indices. This gives the possibility of determining a predicted range of movement of an interest rate index with a unique restriction imposed by the issuer; this restriction is the bandwidth. The investor may position the bandwidth wherever he wishes for the period the investment is valid. In short, this is a structure where the principal is guaranteed, whereas the final interest depends on the level of success the investor has in the reference index movement. This falls within a range preset by the investor, which is restricted more by width than its relative position.

The maturity date is usually short term, about a year, and is issued by guaranteeing the principal.

$$\text{Payoff} = \max(0, D_{\text{success}} \times r_x/365)$$

or alternatively

$$\text{Payoff} = D_{\text{success}} \times \frac{r_x}{365} + (D_{\text{total}} - D_{\text{success}}) \times \frac{\text{rebate}}{365}$$

Figure 16.1 shows the payoff diagram.

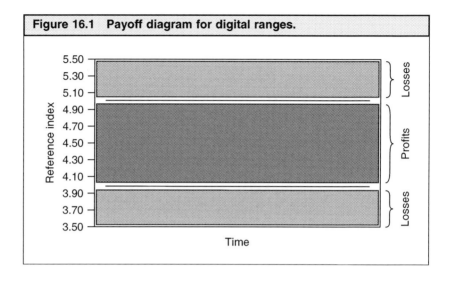

Figure 16.1   Payoff diagram for digital ranges.

Risks

This structure is determined by a basic risk in interest rates and volatility.

For the investor

Whoever buys this structure is determining some stable expectations within the underlying asset. In this case it means interest rates in the money market represented by any index (Euribor, Libor, etc.). Maximisation of profits occurs with stable rates within the preset range, by virtue of the fact that the investor chooses a position to sell the volatility. The risk emerges where there is volatility, which brings the reference rate outside the band preset by the same investor at the start of the operation.

For the issuer

If the rates remain stable within the range, the issuer would be negatively affected. This leads the issuer to take on a final cost of capital that is greater than the cost of capital received initially. In short, where he has not taken out hedging for the structure, the issuer is in a speculative position with high volatility and he would be harmed when the operation ends if, during this whole period, the reference index were to remain stable within the range. He would end up with expired options out of the money (OTM) and pay a higher than market rate.

Construction

Despite all appearances to the contrary – very usual in this type of structure – the issuer of an interest rate corridor note takes from the investor an interest rate deposit r_x higher than the market level r_m, at the time when he receives from him some digital options. In fact, the structure is a deposit with an extra rate for the issuer, $r_x - r_m$, and in fact he should therefore keep account of this. The consideration for this surcharge are options obtained from the investor:

- Digital calls with strike equal to the higher band level chosen by the investor and with payoff $= r_x/365 \times$ notional
- Digital puts with strike equal to the lower band level chosen by the investor and with payoff $= r_x/365 \times$ notional

The numbers of calls and puts are given by the working days of interest calculated during the investment period. For one year there would be 250 calls and 250 puts.

The principal will only be guaranteed where the present value alone from this one-year notional is invested. Within that period, this will obtain the same principal as the investor handed the issuer at the start of the investment.

Where the issuer offers the investor a consolation return or rebate, by each day that the reference index falls outside the band instead of 0%, the structure will incorporate a 'set' of another 250 digital calls and another 250 digital puts (per annum). Now, these options would be for the investor's benefit with daily payoff (for settlement at maturity) equal to this offered rebate. In this way, this whole structure would have 500 options (per annum) for the issuer with payoff equal to the rate offered on the structure, and 500 for the investor with payoff equal to the rebate.

Example

Let's assume that a corridor note structure offers 5.50% (in proportion to each of the 365 investment days), for each day on which the one-year deposit index, e.g. 12 month Euribor, is situated within a maximum band of 0.50%, chosen wherever the investor wishes. For each day that the reference index is outside the band, the investor accrues 0% interest. The standard market deposit interest rate is 4.50%. The investor's choice of where to position the predicted, fluctuating band will depend on future expectations for the 12 month rate each day throughout the investment period. Final interest settlement will take place when the operation matures at the end of one year.

Indicative terms

Description	Deposit in euros with high return linked to 12 month Euribor
Nominal	€10 000 000
Issue price	100%
Interest	5.50% daily for each day, on which 12 month Euribor is situated within a band preset by the customer at the start of the operation. Maximum bandwidth will be 50bp. Where the index falls outside the band, 0% interest accrues for each day this occurs. The successes/errors on Fridays are calculated for 3 days. Accumulated interest is payable on maturity
Term	1 year
Amortisation	100%

Let's assume that the investor chooses to place the band at 4.25% to 4.75% (very central compared to the current level) and invests €10 million nominal. Hypothetically speaking, the issuer receives on the structure, from the investor 250 digital calls at 4.75% with payoff 5.50%/365 and 250 digital puts at 4.25% with the same payoff. The maturity dates of each of the 250 calls and puts correspond to each of the future days on which the index position will be assessed with regard to the bands chosen, namely all working days since the start until one year on.

Where the index is situated within strikes, the investor would strengthen the 5.50%, or equally, the options for the issuer would expire out of the money. Where the index is situated above or below the band limits, the issuer would exercise his options by removing profit from the structure. In the extreme case where the index is situated below or above the bands from the first investment day until the last, exercising all options would bring the issuer 5.50% over 365 days. This would be the interest that he would not pay the investor; the investor would obtain only the nominal invested.

Consider how the issuer would handle this. With the nominal obtained (100%), he will have to invest the present nominal value at the 365 day market interest rate, which in our example is $10\,000\,000/(1 + 4.50\%) = €9\,569\,378$. The objective of this operation is to cover the risk of the deposit interest rate he has taken, or in short, to be assured that the principal will still be there in one year's time for refunding to the investor. Right now, the issuer is taking on a risk for the underlying and volatility, through which, on maturity, where the investor has been successful on the preset bands, he will have to assume payment of higher than market interest. This means there is the possibility to handle this risk or to cancel it.

Eventual success on the bands set by the investor would assume that the options received by the issuer would have expired out of the money. The simplest way to cancel or close this risk would be for the issuer to sell on the market the 250 digital calls and 250 puts with payoff at 5.50%/365 received on the structure he has issued. The strikes should be the same, namely 4.25% for the puts and 4.75% for the calls. With this, the issuer would generate profits where the rates finish within the range. Those profits would not come to more than the value of the options sold. However, there would only be a net profit on the whole structure covered if the value obtained through the sale of these options on the market were higher than attributed to the options received from the investor.

Logically, the underlying of the options sold on the market should also be the 12 month forward rates for each of the following 365 days of the year. Financing of these options for the issuer will arise from that part of the nominal remaining from investment in the standard deposit mentioned earlier. In our case, $100 - 95.69 = 4.31\%$ would be the maximum ready money available to purchase the options. In reality, the issuer's profit might be given through the possibility to buy these options at an amount lower than 4.31%.

Valuation

Valuation of the structure's components is reduced to an interbank deposit at a rate higher than market rate, r_x, along with digital options. Digital options may be European options, whose final payoff is given by a preset quantity rather than by the difference between the final underlying asset and the strike price (call), or vice versa (put). We can follow an analysis based on the Black–Scholes framework. We can valuate the digital options given the option profile, which has no bearing on the relationship between the underlying strike and the final payoff decision, where it expires in the money (ITM).

$$\text{Call} = Xe^{-rT}N(d) \tag{16.1}$$

$$\text{Put} = Xe^{-rT}N(-d) \tag{16.2}$$

with

$$d = \frac{\ln(S/K) + (b - \sigma^2)T}{\sigma\sqrt{T}}$$

where

S = underlying price
K = strike
X = payoff

σ = volatility
r = risk-free interest rate
q = dividend
b = net cost of carry = $r - q$
T = time to option maturity in years

These equations will require a small adjustment. The model assumes the payoff turns into ready cash (where it expires ITM) when the option matures. In the structure, all the payoffs in all options turn into ready cash when the structure matures. This means we must take Xe^{-rT} and multiply it by e^{zT_f} where z is the interest rate that applies to the existing period between the option maturity date and the structure. Within the structure, the issuer implicitly receives options, in exchange for which he issues a deposit with an extra rate $r_x - r_m$.

In a position of financial equilibrium, at the moment the structure is created, the spread over market rates promised by the issuer to the investor only in case of a successful movement of the index inside the band, must be equal to the value of the 500 digital options, implicitly received by the investor.

Consequently, valuation of this structure, at market prices, is reduced to finding the value in the offered extra rate where there is success every day (remember that interest is paid at the end of the period), and the value of the 250 digital calls (with higher-limit strike) and 250 digital puts (with lower-limit strike) with fixed payoff equal to rate r_x is offered on the structure. At the outset, these options owe value equal to the value in the extra rate:

$$r_x - r_m$$

$$= \sum_{i=1}^{n} \left[\underset{\text{payoff} = r_x/365}{\text{digital call } (K = \text{higher limit})} + \underset{\text{payoff} = r_x/365}{\text{digital puts } (K = \text{lower limit})} \right]$$

where n is the number of working days during the life of the structure. The price of the structure at any moment will be given by

$$\text{Price} = \text{present value}(1 + r_x)$$

$$- \sum_{i=1}^{n} \left[\underset{\text{payoff} = r_x/365}{\text{digital call } (K = \text{higher limit})} + \underset{\text{payoff} = r_x/365}{\text{digital puts } (K = \text{lower limit})} \right]$$

$$+ \sum_{i=1}^{n} \left[\underset{\text{payoff} = r_{\text{rebate}}/365}{\text{digital call } (K = \text{higher limit})} + \underset{\text{payoff} = r_{\text{rebate}}/365}{\text{digital puts } (K = \text{lower limit})} \right]$$

$$- \text{present value} \left(\frac{(r_x - r_{\text{rebate}}) \times \text{days observed outside band}}{365} \right)$$

17

STEP-UP CALLABLE

Definition and commercial presentation

A step-up bond is a medium- or long-term bond with fixed but distinct coupons which increase over time. Therefore, an initial annual return is offered over a time period throughout which the issuer can amortise, or easily continue, until the 'original maturity date' of the structure, and pay a coupon higher than previously. By definition, there will be at least two interest periods, namely, two distinct levels of coupon payments. The issuer's opportunities to amortise coincide, at least, with dates where there is a change of coupon. Within this structure, the anticipated amortisation may be established as only on any date set over the life of the operation, at any moment, or throughout the operation, but it must occur punctually on those dates.

Different types of option will produce different types of amortisation.

- European option: amortisation only on a fixed date
- American option: amortisation throughout the whole life of the structure
- Bermudan option: amortisation throughout the life but on preset dates

In this chapter we will confine ourselves to amortisation on one fixed date.

A step-up callable usually has a long-term maturity date of about 10 or 20 years; it is issued by adjusting the price according to the coupons offered, and by guaranteeing the principal:

$$\text{Payoff} = \text{coupons}_X + (\text{coupons}_Y)_{\text{issuer's amortisation}} + \text{principal}$$

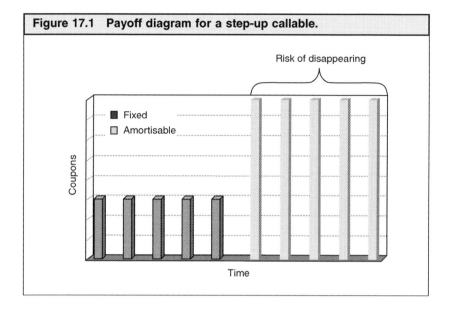

Figure 17.1 Payoff diagram for a step-up callable.

where

X = initial period
Y = a later period presented, at the start, for the amortisation
     anticipated by the issuer

Figure 17.1 shows the payoff diagram.

Risks

The investor in this type of structure assumes a risk for the interest rate
and volatility. Bear in mind that the investor is offered a coupon at slightly
higher than market rate, although this has a stable profile throughout the
life. This creates a penalty where there are rises, and leaves potentially no
investment where there are falls in profitability, starting from the date the
issuer might carry out amortisation. Anyone who invests in a step-up with
issuer amortisation will encounter these specific risks:

- Rise in interest rates above the options offered for the first period (assuming
  purchase is made at par). In this case, he would lose the cost of the
  investment opportunity in a market which has better returns.
- A significant rise in interest rates above the coupons offered for the second
  period (assuming purchase is made at par). In this case, he would lose the
  cost of the investment opportunity in a market which has better returns.

- Reduction in interest rates over the second period. The investor will know, in this case, that the issuer will amortise beforehand and have to reinvest at lower market rates.

Construction

The issuer of the step-up callable issues a fixed coupon bond and acquires a call swaption. This is an IRS put (called receiver) with maturity date equal to the start of the second interest period, and underlying equal to the remaining life from that moment. The strike will be the same as the rate offered on that second interest period. In conditions of perfect equilibrium, the bond issue price should be equal to the present value in all the bond's cash flows, assuming that the title is maintained until its final amortisation date, less the value of the interest rate option, which the issue receives implicitly when the right is reserved beforehand to amortise.

The way this right can be brought about by the issuer is to choose, implicitly in the structure, potential cancellation of the primary obligation to pay interest on the second period, when the higher coupon then comes into force. This action can be carried out (where there is an option to amortise only on the date the coupon changes) through the implicit delivery from the investor to the issuer of a swaption. This allows the investor the potential, on the coupon change date, to collect the fixed rate. And this means a receiver or call swaption. In this way, if he decided to amortise the bond beforehand, through refunding the principal, he would then cancel his interest obligations by exercising the call swaption.

Here the strike will be equal to the interest set for the second period, at the moment the title was issued. So the investor's primary interest obligation is compensated by exercising the option on the part of the issuer, by the same interest, against the investor. Logically, this exercise would only be carried out when, on the date the option matures (start of the second interest period of the structure), the market rates are below the option strike (coupon of the new period), so that by amortising, the issuer would get finance on the market at lower rates for the remaining period of the original structure.

Example

There is a 10 year step-up which pays 5% per annum for the first 5 years and 6% for the remaining period, with the issuer having the option to amortise at the end of the fifth year.

Indicative terms

Description	Bond in euros with fixed coupons different in two periods of time and with the issuer having the option to amortise at the start of the second period
Nominal	€100 000
Issue price	94.95%
Interest	Fixed for period 1: 5% per annum for the first 5 years
	Fixed for period 2: 6% per annum for the last 5 years
	Basis: Act/360
Term	10 years
Amortisation	100% at the end of the tenth year or 100% at the end of the fifth year if the issuer decided to amortise in advance

The structure consists of a bond issue with all the flows offered until the tenth year as if no amortising option existed. At the same time, the issuer receives from the investor a call swaption 5-5 with 6% strike, which gives him the right potentially to collect 6% from the fifth year onward, where he exercises this right. With this, he would cancel his original interest obligation to the investor, and would have to refund the principal in these circumstances. This would be consistent where the interest rates were heading downward. The financing required would be taken at lower market rates, in a new fixed or variable rate issue, according to his future expectations at that moment. Given an interest rate curve (with its corresponding discount factors), the bond issue price without amortising option would be 95.96% (Table 17.1).

To valuate the real structure, namely the breakeven price which the investor has to pay, the value of a 5-5 call swaption with 6% strike at market conditions would have to be deducted from the previous value. Given the same curve,

Table 17.1

Years	Factor	Flow (€)	Present value (€)
1	0.96042	5.00	4.80
2	0.91209	5.00	4.56
3	0.86245	5.00	4.31
4	0.81286	5.00	4.06
5	0.76135	5.00	3.81
6	0.71859	6.00	4.31
7	0.67350	6.00	4.04
8	0.63053	6.00	3.78
9	0.59095	6.00	3.55
10	0.55409	106.00	58.73
		Price	95.96

a 5-5-forward swap rate at 6.54% and an implied market volatility for this swaption at 17%, the call swaption (IRS put) would be worth 1.51% over nominal. This value has been found using the Black–Scholes model. In this way, the cash or cash expenditure, which the investor should achieve through the bond with amortising option, anticipated at the end of the fifth year, on the part of the issuer, would be $95.96 - 1.51 = 94.95\%$ of nominal.

Valuation

Using this type of increasing coupon bond, the only way for the issuer to achieve the amortising option in advance is by introducing, for his own benefit, the option that will give him the right to collect the same fixed rate which he determines for the second interest period in the structure. The second period is where the investor obtains the step-up, or increase in initial coupon towards a higher one. The investor is therefore paying the price quoted on the structure in cash plus the delivery of a call swaption (IRS put), which grants the issuer the right to collect a fixed rate, namely, to offset his interest payment obligations for the period in which the increase in coupons comes into force. Logically, this right will only be exercised if, on the appointed date, the market interest rates for the remaining life of the title are lower than determined by the bond for the second interest period.

From the investor's viewpoint, we can take the valuation of a step-up bond with amortising option and reduce it to three stages:

- Find the value in all the bond flows, assuming there is no amortising option
- Find the value of the corresponding call swaption
- The bond price will equal the difference between the two values

From taking an anticipated amortisation on a set date, namely a European-style strike, the value of the swaption may be found through the Black 76 model. The forward IRS put (call swaption) will be equal to

$$P = e^{-rT}[-F_S N(-d_1) + KN(-d_2)] \qquad (17.1)$$

$$d_1 = \frac{\ln(F_S/K)}{\sigma\sqrt{T}} + \frac{1}{2}\sigma\sqrt{T}$$

$$d_2 = d_1 - \sigma\sqrt{T} \qquad (17.2)$$

where

F_S = underlying: forward swap
K = strike
σ = volatility

r = risk-free interest rate
T = time to option maturity in years
P = put value

The value of the put as calculated above is expressed in terms of the underlying IRS spread. To convert this into a percentage over notional, we write

$$\text{Value over notional } (\%) = \sum_{i=1}^{n} \text{spread value} \times \frac{D_i}{D_b} \times \frac{DF_i}{DF_0} \qquad (17.3)$$

where

D_i = days of interest accrued
D_b = base days by convention
DF_i = discount factor for flow i
DF_0 = discount factor from start of the forward swap

The structure's value will be given by

Price = present value(future bond flows without anticipated amortisation)

   $-$ call swaption(forward swap, strike = higher coupon,

      implied volatility, interest rate, time)

18

RESET NOTE

Definition and commercial presentation

A reset note is a medium- or long-term bond with one or more coupons already fixed (the following options will be fixed at some time in the future according to a reference index), and it usually has a medium maturity of about 5 or 10 years. It is usually issued at par, or adjusted with regard to the coupons set. It guarantees the principal but not coupons that are yet to be determined for issue.

$$\text{Payoff} = 0 < (\text{reference index} - \text{fixed rate}) \times \text{percent}$$

$$< \text{maximum rate} + \text{principal}$$

where percent is a percentage to be determined in the structure depending on market conditions. Figure 18.1 shows the payoff diagram.

Risks

The investor assumes a risk for interest rate and volatility, although these are very slight. Even if the investor is offered an initial coupon with a rate slightly higher than market rate, to make the bond more attractive, there is uncertainty over later coupons, determined by the reference index movement. This represents a threat, through reductions in interest rates below the forward rates, which the market discounts naturally at the moment the title is acquired. The investor in a reset note comes up against the following specific risks:

- Reduction in reference index interest rates below the forward rates, which the market discounts, at the moment the title is acquired, for the remaining life of the title, through payment of the coupon or fixed coupons.

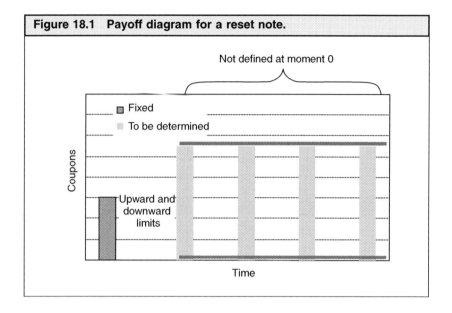

Figure 18.1   Payoff diagram for a reset note.

- Depending on the limits set, there may be a small risk in upward or downward volatility (see later).

Construction

The issuer of a reset note issues a bond with the first coupon or coupons set and acquires a swaption spread, which may be a call or put. This depends on whether there is a desire to give the structure a bias, bearing in mind any commercial interest. More usually, where a bias is given to an upward movement in interest rates, to attract the investor, this usually means a put swaption spread is involved. The investor receives from the issuer an IRS call, namely, a put swaption with a strike lower than the put swaption handed to the issuer. The spread for the investor is determined by a profile like Figure 18.2.

Where there are conditions of perfect equilibrium, the bond issue price should be equal to the present value in all the fixed cash flows, plus the differential of the value of the options involved in the structure. The formula for determining the interest is

$$0 < (\text{reference index} - \text{fixed rate}) \times \text{percent} < \text{maximum rate}$$

The reference index will usually be an IRS rate, which is the fixed rate and which may be adjusted in slightly lower than market conditions, whereas percent is determined by the interest differential gearing. The fixed rate in the

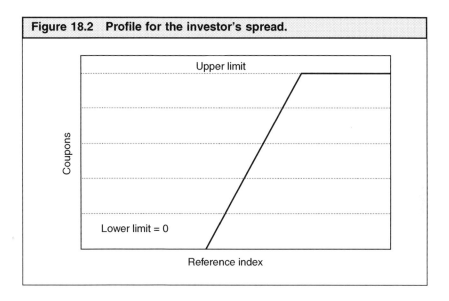

Figure 18.2 Profile for the investor's spread.

equation consists of the lower put swaption strike and the maximum rate the investor will collect by the higher put swaption strike that the issuer receives from the structure.

Example

There is a 3 year reset note paying 5% per annum for the first year. The interest for the remaining 2 years will be determined by the lowest formula, which leaves it set between 0% and a maximum of 8.485%. The principal is guaranteed.

Indicative terms

Description	Bond in euros with first coupon set; the other coupons will be set at the end of one year for the rest of the bond's life, according to the equation on page 140. Interest will be set between 0% and 8.485%
Nominal	€100 000 000
Issue price	100.00%
Interest	Fixed for period 1: 5% per annum for 1 year
	Fixed for period 2: payable every year Act/Act
Term	3 years
Amortisation	100.00%

The structure consists of a bond issue with the first flow fixed at 5%. This rate is approximately the market interest rate according to the curve used (Table 18.1). For the remaining coupons, under equilibrium conditions, the investor must be offered a value equivalent to the present value in the last two flows (assuming they are annual flows) of a 3 year bond, namely 5.42% for an interbank risk (Table 18.1). This leads to Table 18.2.

The investor will be due to receive a swaption whose value is €9 498 392 greater than he will deliver, under complete financial equilibrium (assuming the issuer does not obtain profits from the operation). In this example the swap between issuer and investor of two put swaptions with strikes 4.70%

Table 18.1			
Term	Actual days	Par rate	Discount factor
O/N	1	5.00	0.9998611
T/N	3	4.35	0.9996196
1 day	6	4.35	0.9992573
1 week	10	4.38	0.9987689
1 month	34	4.46	0.9957951
2 months	64	4.54	0.9919884
3 months	97	4.46	0.9881124
4 months	125	4.56	0.9844223
5 months	156	4.66	0.9802025
6 months	188	4.77	0.9757026
7 months	216	4.81	0.9719330
8 months	246	4.86	0.9678542
9 months	276	4.91	0.9637357
10 months	307	4.95	0.9594896
11 months	337	4.99	0.9553518
1 year	370	5.04	0.9507690
2 years	734	5.32	0.9009597
3 years	1098	5.42	0.8531293
4 years	1464	5.49	0.8068067
5 years	1829	5.56	0.7619415

Note: the rates of terms higher than 1 year correspond to an IRS whose fixed rate is paid annually against a six-monthly floating.

Table 18.2			
	Coupon	Flow (€)	Discount factor	Present value of flow (€)
Year 2	5.415	5 415 000	0.9009597	4 878 697
Year 3	5.415	5 415 000	0.8531293	4 619 695
			Total	9 498 392

and 5.50%, respectively, will generate a difference of €9 498 355. Even if the nominal from each structure's title is €100 000 000, then the nominal amounts of the swaptions are €1060.70 million, owing to the gearing in the structure. The nominal amounts necessary to fit the formula for determining the interest are given by

$$\text{nominal} \times \text{percentage from the interest equation} \times 100$$

In our case this means 100 million × 10.607% × 100 = €1 060 700 000 for each swaption. The strike swaption at 4.70% is the swaption which the investor receives in exchange for delivering the 5.50%. The volatilities used in the valuation with the Black 76 model have been set at 17% for the put swaption at 4.70% strike, and at 18% for the put swaption at 5.50% strike. Using these volatilities and the rates curve of Table 18.1, the values of the swaptions are as follows:

- Put swaption with strike at 4.70%: value €17 587 846
- Put swaption with strike at 5.50%: value €8 089 490

The difference is exactly €9 498 355, which has practically the same present value as the last 3 year coupons at market conditions. To verify that the fixed nominal figures of the swaptions are correct and generate the expected payoffs, let's look at two possible cases.

Case A

Suppose the 2 year IRS rate were 5.10% in year 1, then the interest would be fixed at (5.10 − 4.70) × 10.607% = 4.243% (interest to be collected at the end of years 2 and 3). On a nominal of €100 million, the result is €4 242 800. It may be shown that the investor's swaption strike at 4.70% with a nominal of €1060.7 million does indeed generate (5.10% − 4.70%) × 1060.7 million = €4 242 800 for each of the underlying IRS years (years 2 and 3). The structure would generate the following cash flows:

- Year 1 = 5%
- Year 2 = 4.24%
- Year 3 = 4.24%

Case B

Suppose the 2 year IRS rate were 6.00% in year 1, then the interest would be fixed at (6.00 − 4.70) × 10.607% = 13.79%. Since it is set at a rate of 8.485%, then 8.485% will be collected. On a nominal of €100 million, the result is €8 485 000. Now we will show the results generated by the investor's swaption strike at 4.70% and the issuer's swaption strike at 5.50%. Both have nominal figures of €1060.27 million:

- Investor's swaption: (6.0% − 4.70%) × 1060.27 million = €13 783 510
- Issuer's swaption: (6.0% − 5.50%) × 1060.27 million = €5 301 350

The difference for the investor is €8 482 160, or 8.48% of the structure's annual interest rate for years 2 and 3. The structure would generate the following cash flows:

- Year 1 = 5%
- Year 2 = 8.48%
- Year 3 = 8.48%

Valuation

Step 1

If the fixed coupon or coupons were higher or lower than the corresponding ones at actual market conditions, then the difference must be found for these coupons at present value.

Step 2

Find the present value at market conditions for the coupons that are not fixed.

Step 3

Find the value for each of the two put swaptions (interest rate calls). The value of the lower strike corresponds to the investor, and the other value corresponds to the issuer. The nominal figures of the two swaptions are equal and do not correspond to the structure's nominal. The latter must be calculated as follows:

$$\text{structure's nominal} \times IDG \times 100.$$

where IDG is the interest differential gearing or percentage participation of the interest index difference in the formula.

$$C = e^{-rT}[F_S N(-d_1) - KN(-d_2)] \tag{18.1}$$

$$d_1 = \frac{\ln(F_S/K)}{\sigma\sqrt{T}} + \frac{1}{2}\sigma\sqrt{T}$$

$$d_2 = d_1 - \sigma\sqrt{T} \tag{18.2}$$

where

F_S = underlying: forward swap
K = strike

σ = volatility
r = risk-free interest rate
T = time to option maturity in years
C = call value

The value of the call, calculated in this way, would be expressed in terms of underlying IRS spread. To convert into percentage over notional, we write

$$\text{Value over notional (\%)} = \sum_{i=1}^{n} \text{spread value} \times \frac{D_i}{D_b} \times \frac{DF_i}{DF_0} \qquad (18.3)$$

where

D_i = days of interest accrued
D_b = base days by convention
DF_i = discount factor for flow i
DF_0 = discount factor from start of the forward swap

The structure's value will be given by

Price = present value in overvaluation of the bond's future flows already fixed

+ put swaption(forward swap, lower strike, implied volatility,

interest rate, time)

− put swaption(forward swap, higher strike, implied volatility,

interest rate, time)

+ present value in the principal

Present value in overvaluation of the bond's future flows already fixed will have a positive sign where there is overvaluation and a negative sign where there is undervaluation. It will be zero where there are fixed flows with interest rates at market conditions.

19

PARTICIPATING SWAP

Definition and commercial presentation

This is an interest rate structure through which those taking out funds at variable rates may transfer their financing to a fixed rate which, even if it were higher than the standard market rate, would also allow them to use eventual reductions in interest rates. The buyer pays a maximum fixed interest unless there is a reduction in rates, in which case he will pay market rates (floating tranche). In short, fixed interest is paid where there are rises in rates, but with the possibility that variable rates might be paid in bearish situations. Logically, this will be when the changeover offers more interest. It has the advantage of a purchased IRS on which there is a fixed payment rate (higher than standard market rate) and the advantage of paying the variable rate when there are reductions, although only managing to capture part of the reductions.

Usually maturity is medium and long term from 5 to 30 years. Participating swaps are not investment vehicles per se. Their role, as structured derivatives to be managed, is the conversion or limiting of interest rate movements that may affect any real investment or financing operation.

$$\text{Payoff} = \begin{cases} (T_r - x\%) & \text{if } T_r > \text{limit rate} \\ (T_r - x\%) + T_r + (\text{limit rate} - T_r) \times A\% & \text{if } F_r < \text{threshold rate} \end{cases}$$

where

$x\%$ = participating swap rate
$A\%$ = percentage of participation in the floating tranche

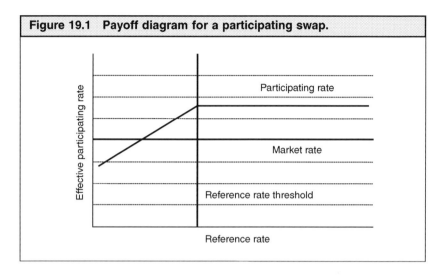

Figure 19.1   Payoff diagram for a participating swap.

T_r = money market reference rate (Euribor, Libor, etc.)
F_r = market reference floating rate

The threshold rate is the interest rate below which the buyer would pay floating interest. The rates position is evaluated on the date the rates are set. Figure 19.1 shows the payoff diagram.

Risks

The buyer must be someone taking out funds, and is using this structured swap to try to limit the financial cost from an eventual rise in interest rates. This is assuming a fixed rate somewhat higher than market level, although with the possibility of moving to floating rates, also slightly higher than the market rates, if there are falls. In this way, the greatest risk is that there occur only rate rises. In this case, even if only the participating rate is paid, the participating rate is somewhat higher than the alternative of a standard IRS. On the other hand, eventual large reductions in rates would encourage the buyer to pay variable rates, although this would be without seizing the full 100% from these falls. Reductions in market rates reduce the interest to be paid, but this becomes smaller each time it occurs.

In short, whoever acquires this structured swap assumes the advantages and disadvantages of paying fixed and floating rates in a combined way. This is determining some mixed expectations between bullish and moderately bearish for the underlying asset interest rates, with respect to the initial levels. In addition, where reductions in interest rates occur, there is a benefit from increased volatility in the interest rates. The greatest advantages for the buyer are seen in the measure with which a duality in its financing structure pays fixed rates, where there are interest rises, and pays variable rates in bearish situations. However, this 'great convenience' is paid for in terms of slightly higher rates than the standard rates in both cases.

Construction

This is a structure in which the buyer acquires an IRS (pays fixed and receives floating) through a nominal N, and simultaneously receives from the issuer a floor in a nominal that is a percentage of N. The floor strike is the reference threshold which marks two possible rates of payoff determined in the participating swap. The buyer tackles the floor cost by assuming a fixed swap rate initially higher than the market level. This rate, however, will be the maximum payable in any situation. Where there are reductions, the buyer will not see the benefits at 100% of these reductions, unless he does this in a decreasing way.

Example

There is a 3 year participating swap floating against fixed rate per annum, in both cases, for which the buyer has paid a fixed rate of 5.78% (the market rate of a standard IRS is 5.413%), whereas the 1 year rate (12 month Euribor) is above this rate (5.78%). If the 1 year rate were to be below this, then the buyer would pay the floating rate, although he is only affected by 50% of the fall. The reference nominal of the participating swap is €100 million.

Indicative terms

Description	Interest rate swap in euros on which the person paying the fixed rate (per annum) pays 5.78% if 12 month Euribor is above 5.78%. Beneath this he pays a floating rate that will be determined later on
Nominal	€100 000 000
Interest on each date of fixing (for investor)	If 12 month Euribor > 5.78%, he pays 5.78% and receives 12 month Euribor. Cost of financing is 5.78%
	If 12 month Euribor < 5.78%, he pays 12 month Euribor + (5.78% − 12 month Euribor) × 50%, and receives 12 month Euribor. Cost of financing is Euribor + 50% of the reduction in respect of the 5.78%
	Both branches are paid annually: fixed branch 30/360, variable branch Act/360
Term	3 years

The structure consists of a 3 year IRS on which the buyer pays a fixed rate (5.78%) higher than the market rate at standard conditions (5.41%) and receives 12 month Euribor if 12 month Euribor exceeds 5.78%. This greater cost is because the IRS buyer receives a strike floor at 5.78% of 50% nominal of the IRS, namely €50 million. The role of the floor received by the buyer is to allow reductions in interest rates that enable him to benefit in spite of paying the fixed rate on the IRS. However, the falls are only seized on 50% of its rise beyond 5.78%. Above this level, the buyer knows that he has a limit on interest payments at this 5.78% rate.

To evaluate this structure, we must find the value of the floor over the term of the operation. Table 19.1 gives the interest rate curve. To evaluate the floor, we use a 3 year implied volatility at 15.50%, since in the IRS of the three variable flows per annum, the first is fixed at the moment of the agreement, through which the floor must only cover the 1 year rate within one year and then within two. This assumes it must only contain two 12 month rate floorlets or puts. We now have Table 19.2.

The interest rate spread will be given by

$$\text{Spread} = \text{value} \Big/ \sum_{i=1}^{m} \text{YF}_i \times \text{DF}_i \times \text{notional}$$

Table 19.1

Term	Actual days	Par rate	Discount factor
O/N	3	5.00	0.9995835
T/N	5	4.35	0.9993420
1 day	6	4.35	0.9992213
1 week	12	4.38	0.9984916
1 month	38	4.46	0.9952730
2 months	67	4.54	0.9915889
3 months	97	4.46	0.9880801
4 months	129	4.57	0.9838623
5 months	158	4.67	0.9799118
6 months	189	4.77	0.9755579
7 months	220	4.82	0.9713898
8 months	248	4.86	0.9675886
9 months	279	4.91	0.9633414
10 months	311	4.96	0.9589477
11 months	340	5.00	0.9549363
1 year	370	5.04	0.9507583
2 years	735	5.32	0.9008371
3 years	1102	5.42	0.8526506
4 years	1466	5.49	0.8065834

Note: the rates of terms higher than 1 year correspond to an IRS whose fixed rate is paid annually against a six-monthly floating.

Table 19.2

Date	Zero rate (365)	Forward rate (360)	European floor strike 5.78%	
			European value	Cash value (€)
Today			15.50%	(volatility)
1 year	5.104	5.46	0.480	244 852
2 years	5.322	5.54	0.534	270 098
3 years	5.420			
			Total	514 951

where

YF = fraction of year in which it is accrued
DF = discount factor
m = number of flows

And we get Table 19.3. In our example

$$\text{Spread} = \frac{514\,951}{137\,204\,210} = 0.37\%$$

If we add 0.37% to the standard IRS market rate of 5.41%, the result is 5.78%; this is the participating rate that the IRS buyer would take on for 12 month Euribor rates higher than 5.78%. In short, the buyer limits his financing cost where there are rises, and gets a part profit from reductions. For this, he assumes a fixed cost that is slightly greater than for the standard IRS.

Valuation

Valuation of the participating swap is reduced to calculating the IRS value at a higher than market rate, and the floor the buyer receives for managing to get a part profit from potential interest rate reductions.

The option value the buyer receives is the value he allows the issuer to offer for participation up to the first of the rate reductions. This is in spite of

Table 19.3

	Year fraction	Factor	Notional (€)	Product (€)
1 year	1.0194	0.9511752	50 000 000	48 483 515
2 years	1.0111	0.9013697	50 000 000	45 569 248
3 years	1.0111	0.8535451	50 000 000	43 151 447
			Total	137 204 210

the issuer having the commitment on the IRS to pay a higher than market rate at standard conditions. The value of the European floor is given by equations (15.1) and (15.3).

The value of the structure from the holder's viewpoint (the person who will pay the participating swap rate) will be given by

Price = IRS value at agreed fixed rate (higher than market standard)

− floor[underlying(r_{imp_i}), strike (IRS participating rate),

time$_i$, r_i, volatility]

where

r = risk-free interest rate
r_{imp} = implicit interest rate

The nominal of the floor will be x% of the nominal of the IRS. Alternatively, in interest rate terms, the participating equilibrium rate will be given by

Participating rate = market IRS rate + value in floor spread[underlying(r_{imp_i}),

strike (IRS participating rate), time$_i$, r_i, volatility]

20

PERFORMANCE SWAP

Definition and commercial presentation

The performance swap is an interest structure for the agent taking out funds so that on an IRS he obtains financing rates lower than the market level. This is whenever the interest rates fail to reach certain levels. Specifically, the buyer pays a fixed interest, lower than the market level, if on the day the IRS interest is fixed, for the corresponding period, the reference index has not reached a determined level, normally higher than the starting level. This gives a particularly interesting result where there are low interest rates and the interest rate curves have a positive slope.

Maturity is usually medium and long term, from 5 to 10 years. These structures deal more with risk management than with investment or financing. The target objective for whoever acquires it is to convert the interest risks from an earlier investment or financing operation.

$$
\text{Payoff} = \begin{cases} 0 & \text{if reference rate} > \text{established limit} \\ \text{reference rate} - x\% & \text{if } x\% < \text{reference rate} < \text{established limit} \\ x\% - \text{reference rate} & \text{if reference rate} < x\% \end{cases}
$$

where $x\%$ is the performance swap rate, and reference rate is the market reference floating rate. Figure 20.1 shows the payoff diagram. The assessment of whether the barrier has been reached only occurs on the date interest is fixed, not during the whole period in which interest is accrued.

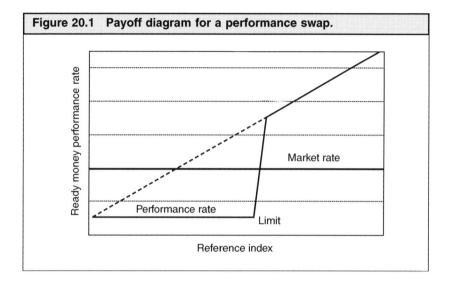

Figure 20.1 Payoff diagram for a performance swap.

Risks

This structure allows financing costs to be reduced, provided the reference index fails to reach set levels. These levels are normally higher than the market. The greatest risk for the buyer is where the comparative advantage disappears. In this case the buyer is the person taking out funds to provide hedging for it. When the 'disallowed' level is reached, the buyer has to assume floating financing costs according to pure market conditions. Therefore, the negative cost of the structure would be given by the difference between the fixed market rate which might have been obtained through a standard IRS and the simple variable rate which it will only assume once the rates have risen and reached the level we call the barrier.

Whoever buys this structure is determining expectations somewhere between bearish and moderately bullish for the underlying asset's interest rates in relation to their starting levels. In reality, stable expectations are determined for limited volatility in the interest rates. The major advantages for the buyer are seen in the extent to which fixed rates are obtained on an IRS, rates which are lower than market rates. This is where there are moderate rises in short-term rates without the barrier levels being reached.

Construction

This structure involves a type of barrier option. The buyer – we cannot speak of an investor here – delivers a financial asset to the issuer; in exchange for this asset, the issuer reduces his fixed financing rate in an IRS. Specifically, the buyer delivers a part-time knock-in cap – a cap whose barrier activation level is limited to the day on which the option matures.

This cap allows the issuer (who receives the fixed rate initially on the IRS) to apply the floating market interest rate. This is where the knock-in level is reached and the option expires in the money. In this way, if activation were to occur, the buyer would then take on a floating interest cost instead of the lower than market swap rate originally offered on the structure. Financially speaking, an up-and-in cap maintains parity with other simple valuation instruments (see later).

Example

There is a 3 year performance swap, annual floating against fixed, in both cases, for which the one paying the fixed rate pays 1.22% below the market rate (5.42%), namely 4.20%, provided that 12 month Euribor is not above 6% at the end of each of the three years. In this case the buyer would pay 12 month Euribor for the relevant period. Let's assume the reference nominal of the performance swap is €10 million.

Indicative terms

Description	Interest rate swap in euros on which the person paying the fixed (annual) rate pays 4.20% (−1.22% below a 3 year market IRS) if 12 month Euribor is below 6%
Nominal	€100 000 000
Interest on each date of fixing (for buyer)	If 12 month Euribor < 4.20%, he pays 4.20% and receives 12 month Euribor. Cost of financing is 4.20%
	If 4.20% < 12 month Euribor < 6%, he pays 4.20% and receives 12 month Euribor. Cost of financing is 4.20%
	If 12 month Euribor > 6%, the swap is cancelled and there is no interest swap. The buyer will come to the market and will get financing according to the conditions existing at that moment. If he makes it variable, his financing cost will be 12 month Euribor
	Use Act/360
Term	3 years

The structure consists of a 3 year IRS on which the buyer pays a fixed rate (4.20%), lower than the market rate at standard conditions (5.42%), and receives 12 month Euribor. In turn, the IRS buyer delivers an up-and-in cap with a strike at 4.20% and a barrier at 6%. The interest swap disappears where 12 month Euribor reaches or exceeds 6% on the day the interest is fixed. In this case, to get the option activated for the issuer, the issuer acquires the right to collect the difference between the rate higher than 6% and the 4% rate. In short, the issuer would collect the total floating rate by collecting the IRS fixed rate of 4.20% plus the difference between the market rate and 4.20%. So, the swap buyer would lose the hedge and pay the floating rate. If, thanks to the cap, the issuer manages to collect the floating rate, and through the IRS had to pay it, the interest swap with the buyer is then cancelled automatically for this period.

As we shall see later on, a knock-in cap may be evaluated through a standard cap with strike equal to the barrier level and a digital cap with strike equal to the barrier (clearly to be bounced back from the barrier) and payoff equal to the difference between the barrier (6%) and the original strike of the knock-in cap (4.20%). In our example we will have

- Standard cap with strike 6%
- Digital cap with strike 6% and payoff 6% − 4.20%

Table 20.1 shows the interest rate curve. To assess the cap we use a 3 year implied volatility at 18%. Table 20.2 shows the results of the valuation. The interest rate spread is given by

$$\text{Spread} = \text{cap value} \bigg/ \sum_{i=1}^{m} \text{YF}_i \times \text{DF}_i \times \text{notional}$$

where

YF = fraction of year in which it is accrued
DF = discount factor
m = number of flows

And we get Table 20.3. In our example

$$\text{Spread} = \frac{335\,285}{27\,440\,842} = 1.22\%$$

It may be shown that the values present in euros for three flows, payable annually over a 3 year period and corresponding to 1.22% on basis Act/360, are €118 479, €111 357 and €105 449.

In short, the issuer could apply a reduction in the fixed rate the buyer has to pay, of 1.22% above market rate. This is at equilibrium, with the knock-in

Table 20.1

Term	Actual days	Par rate	Discount factor
O/N	3	5.00	0.9995835
T/N	5	4.35	0.9993420
1 day	6	4.35	0.9992213
1 week	12	4.38	0.9984916
1 month	38	4.46	0.9952730
2 months	67	4.54	0.9915889
3 months	97	4.46	0.9880801
4 months	129	4.57	0.9838623
5 months	158	4.67	0.9799118
6 months	189	4.77	0.9755579
7 months	220	4.82	0.9713898
8 months	248	4.86	0.9675886
9 months	279	4.91	0.9633414
10 months	311	4.96	0.9589477
11 months	340	5.00	0.9549363
1 year	370	5.04	0.9507583
2 years	735	5.32	0.9008371
3 years	1102	5.42	0.8526506
4 years	1466	5.49	0.8065834

Note: the rates of terms higher than 1 year correspond to an IRS whose fixed rate is paid annually against a six-monthly floating.

Table 20.2

Date	Zero rate (365)	Implicit rate (360)	European cap strike 6%		Digital cap strike 6%	
			European value	Cash value (€)	Digital value	Cash value (€)
Today			18.00%	(volatility)	18.00%	(volatility)
1 year	5.104	5.46	0.189	19 061	0.638	65 047
2 years	5.322	5.54	0.345	34 873	0.795	80 426
3 years	5.420	5.65	0.475	48 005	0.869	87 873
			Total	101 939	Total	233 346

Cap value = €335 285
Nominal = 3.35%

cap valued at €335 285. Considering this is the value of the cap received by the issuer, and deducting the profit being chased by the issuer, the structure should offer this reduction at the fixed rate payable on the IRS. This leads to what we have called the performance swap rate.

Valuation

To valuate the performance swap, we will need to calculate the market IRS value and the up-and-in cap (part-time) which the buyer delivers to obtain

Table 20.3

	Year fraction	Discount factor	Notional (€)	Product (€)
1 year*	1.0194	0.95117521	10 000 000	9 696 703
2 years	1.0111	0.90136975	10 000 000	9 113 850
3 years	1.0111	0.85354513	10 000 000	8 630 290
			Total	27 440 842

*This is considered a leap year.

the performance rate. This is potentially lower than market level for standard IRS operations.

The option value received by the issuer allows him to offer the buyer an initial fixed rate lower than market level. That is subject to the barrier level not being reached on the rate assessment dates, which have to be applied to each period. Note that the barrier option involved is not a standard type, since assessment on whether the barrier has been reached is only made on the date each option matures. However, its valuation proves particularly straightforward. When we observe the knock-in cap with barrier H_0 above the strike K_0, then if we are assessing a standard cap, although with strike K_1 equal to the barrier, it would only be necessary to add a digital cap with strike K_2 equal to the barrier and payoff $H - K_0$.

The value of a part-time knock-in cap (barrier evaluated only at maturity) is given by

$$\text{Standard cap with } K_1 = H + \text{digital cap with } K_1 = H$$
$$(\text{payoff} = H - K_0) \tag{20.1}$$

The standard cap is evaluated using the Black 76 model of equation (14.1). The model for the digital cap is the same as equation (16.1).

The value of the structure from the holder's viewpoint (the holder is the person who will pay the performance swap rate) will be

$$\text{Price} = \text{market IRS value}$$

$$- \text{knock-in cap[underlying}(r_{\text{imp}_i}), \text{strike}(r_{\text{fixed}}),$$

$$\text{barrier, time}_i, r_i, \text{volatility]}$$

where

r = risk-free interest rate
r_{imp} = implicit interest rate

Alternatively, in interest rate terms, the breakeven performance rate will be given by

Performance rate = market IRS rate

$$- \text{value in rate of knock-in cap}[\text{underlying}(r_{\text{imp}_i}),$$

$$\text{strike}(r_{\text{fixed}}), \text{barrier}, \text{time}_i, r_i, \text{volatility}]$$

21

STEP-UP TRIGGERED CAP

Definition and commercial presentation

The step-up triggered cap is an interest rate structure that offers two levels of interest rate rises; this may negatively affect financing if taken at floating rates of interest. Specifically, the buyer pays a variable interest as far as a first ceiling level. Where this ceiling is exceeded by more than a preset amount, the upper limit is shifted to a higher level. The fundamental advantage in this structure is that its initial cost reduces in respect of a standard cap with similar properties. This may prove of particular interest for hedges where interest rates are moderately bullish.

The maturity dates are medium and long term from 3 years up to 15 and 20 years. They are not investment instruments; they are structured derivatives whose role is to convert interest rates without swapping the principal:

$$\text{Payoff} = \begin{cases} 0 & \text{if reference rate} < \text{limit 1} \\ \text{reference rate} - \text{limit 1} & \text{if limit 1} < \text{reference rate} < \text{limit 2} \\ \text{reference rate} - \text{limit 2} & \text{if limit 2} < \text{reference rate} \end{cases}$$

where reference rate is the floating market reference rate, and with limit 1 < limit 2. Valuation of the reference rates, in respect of limits, only occurs on each date the interest is fixed, not during the whole period the interest is accrued. Figure 21.1 shows the payoff diagram.

Risks

This is a structure aimed at generating a cap with certain special features. The fundamental feature is that each time the interest rates are fixed,

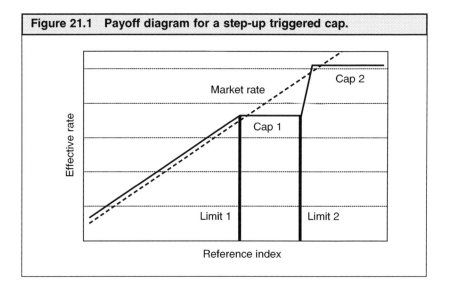

Figure 21.1   Payoff diagram for a step-up triggered cap.

the ceiling is situated at two distinct levels. The lower ceiling is valid whenever the reference index lies between the lower ceiling and the upper ceiling. If the reference index rises beyond the upper ceiling, the real level of protection is moved to a higher level. Another feature is the relative reduction in price that occurs in a standard cap with similar properties.

For the buyer

The structure is composed of two barrier caps (see later). Specifically, the buyer receives, explicitly or implicitly, a knockout cap and a knock-in cap with partial time, that is, whose valuation for deactivation or activation of the barrier is limited to the day on which the option matures. The caps have distinct strikes. The first (knockout) would disappear if it reached the second limit, whereas the second would actually be activated at this point. Consequently, this structure presents a profile of relatively 'unstable' risks, especially in respect of the knockout cap (Figure 21.2). This option's sensitivity to variations in the linked underlying asset (short-term interest rates) can acquire negative or positive values, depending on the relative position of the asset (Figure 21.3). The same goes for sensitivity to volatility of the underlying asset (Figure 21.4).

By also having a knock-in cap, it is possible to alleviate this erratic behaviour in some sensitivity measurements for the knockout cap. In this way, the structure within is seen to benefit predominantly from increases in

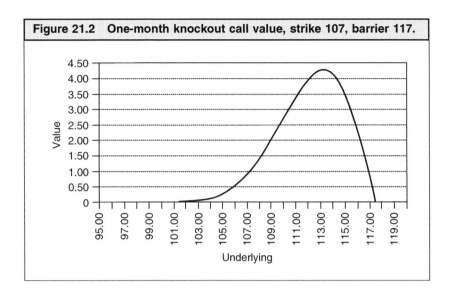

Figure 21.2   One-month knockout call value, strike 107, barrier 117.

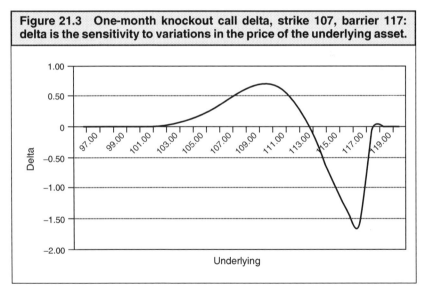

Figure 21.3   One-month knockout call delta, strike 107, barrier 117: delta is the sensitivity to variations in the price of the underlying asset.

volatility and rises in interest rates. However, the most beneficial scenario for the buyer is that both the rises in volatility levels and in interest rates are relatively moderate. Rises which do not go past the second limit will allow the one buying this structure to make the very best of this position.

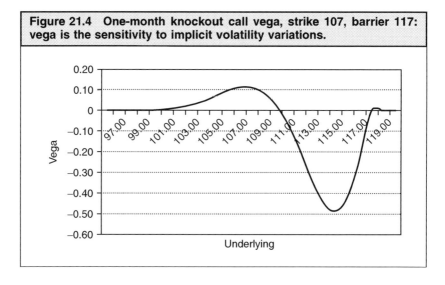

Figure 21.4 One-month knockout call vega, strike 107, barrier 117: vega is the sensitivity to implicit volatility variations.

For the issuer

This structure's major virtue is its low cost. Consequently, the options which the issuer will deliver to the buyer have a lower value than standard options. However, the issuer must arrange a proper hedge, which could be rather more complex, given the unstable nature of the sensitivity parameters of one of its components. Scenarios in which the reference index does not exceed the second limit would create poorer results for an issuer who has hedged the position inadequately. In any case, the sharp price reduction that occurs on the hedge may allow the agent to enjoy a greater profit margin when he values the constituent options. Clearly, management like this is moving away from pure financial design and tending towards commercial aspects and the use of product sophistication to justify greater management margins.

Construction

The step-up triggered cap involves two types of barrier option. The buyer (he is not an investor) receives from the issuer a knockout cap and a knock-in cap with partial time; that is, where the valuations for eventual deactivation or activation of the barriers are limited to the day the option matures (on each date the interest is fixed during the structure's life).

The knockout cap allows the buyer to have upward cover in interest rates with ceiling set at the first limit; the reference index may not pass the second limit. If it did, this caplet would deactivate (a cap consists of *n* caplets) although, at the same time, the knock-in caplet is activated, which moves the hedge level to a higher rate. That higher level is the strike of the knock-in cap.

Example

There is a 3 year step-up triggered cap through which the buyer has a cap at
5.50%, whereas at the end of each of the three years, 12 month Euribor may
not be above 7.50%. If the Euribor were to exceed this, the buyer would have
his ceiling moved to 7.50% for the relevant period. Valuation is made on each
of the three interest periods. Let's assume that the reference nominal of the
step-up triggered cap is €10 million.

Indicative terms

Description	Cap in euros on which the buyer has two levels of upward cover in interest rates linked to 12 month Euribor
Nominal	€10 000 000
Interest on each date of fixing (for buyer)	If 12 month Euribor < limit 1 (5.50%), the buyer collects 0. Cost of financing is 12 month Euribor
	If limit 2 (7.50%) > 12 month Euribor > limit 1 (5.50%), the buyer collects 12 month Euribor − limit 1 (5.50%). Cost of financing is 5.50%
	If 12 month Euribor > limit 2 (7.50%) > limit 1 (5.50%), the buyer collects 12 month Euribor − limit 2 (7.50%)
Term	3 years
Price	€59 359 or 0.22% at 3 year annual spread in three payments

The structure consists in acquiring, on the buyer's part, an up-and-out
cap at strike 5.50% with barrier at 7.50% and an up-and-in cap at strike
7.50% with barrier at 7.50%. Both caps have partial time; that is, valuation of the barrier's deactivation or activation is limited to the date each
option matures, or to the caplet comprising each cap. Both caps may
be summarised in simpler caps. In our example we have the following
results:

● Up-and-out cap at 5.50% with barrier at 7.50% is equivalent to a position on

    European cap with strike 5.50%

       − European cap with strike 7.50%

       − digital cap with strike 7.50%   (payoff = 7.50% − 5.50%)

- Up-and-in cap at 7.50% with barrier at 7.50% is equivalent to a position on European cap with strike 7.50%

Table 21.1 shows the interest curve. To value the cap we use a 3 year implied volatility at 18% for all the options. The purpose of this is to simplify the example, since in fact the corresponding smile should be used, and bearing in mind the corresponding strikes. This effect will clearly have an impact on the valuation, but will not prevent us from checking the important price reduction in respect of a standard option with similar characteristics. As a result of the valuation, we obtain Table 21.2 for the knockout cap and Table 21.3 for the knock-in cap. From the figures in Table 21.4 we can now calculate the interest rate spread using the formula

$$\text{Spread} = \text{value} \bigg/ \sum_{i=1}^{m} \text{YF}_i \times \text{DF}_i \times \text{notional} \qquad (21.1)$$

where

YF = fraction of year in which it is accrued
DF = discount factor
m = number of flows

Table 21.1			
Term	Actual days	Par rate	Discount factor
O/N	3	5.00	0.9995835
T/N	5	4.35	0.9993420
1 day	6	4.35	0.9992213
1 week	12	4.38	0.9984916
1 month	38	4.46	0.9952730
2 months	67	4.54	0.9915889
3 months	97	4.46	0.9880801
4 months	129	4.57	0.9838623
5 months	158	4.67	0.9799118
6 months	189	4.77	0.9755579
7 months	220	4.82	0.9713898
8 months	248	4.86	0.9675886
9 months	279	4.91	0.9633414
10 months	311	4.96	0.9589477
11 months	340	5.00	0.9549363
1 year	370	5.04	0.9507583
2 years	735	5.32	0.9008371
3 years	1102	5.42	0.8526506
4 years	1466	5.49	0.8065834

Note: the rates of terms higher than 1 year correspond to an IRS whose fixed rate is paid annually against a six-monthly floating.

Table 21.2

Date	Zero rate (365)	Implicit rate (360)	European cap strike 5.5%		European cap strike 7.5%		Digital cap strike 7.5%	
			European value	Cash value (€)	European value	Cash value (€)	Digital value	Cash value (€)
Today			18.00%	(volatility)	18.00%	(volatility)	18.00%	(volatility)
1 year	5.104	5.46	0.358	36 201	0.018	1 772	0.113	11 505
2 years	5.322	5.54	0.522	52 762	0.084	8 534	0.332	33 601
3 years	5.420	5.65	0.652	65 884	0.169	17 161	0.496	50 381
			Total	154 847	Total	27 467	Total	95 488

Cap value = €31 892
Nominal = 0.32%

Table 21.3

Date	Zero rate	Implicit rate (360)	European cap strike 7.5%	
			European value	Cash value (€)
Today			18.00%	(volatility)
1 year	5.104	5.46	0.018	1 772
2 years	5.322	5.54	0.084	8 534
3 years	5.420	5.65	0.169	17 161
			Total	27 467

Cap value = €27 467
Nominal = 0.27%

Table 21.4

	Year fraction	Discount factor	Notional (€)	Product (€)
1 year*	1.0194	0.95117521	10 000 000	9 696 703
2 years	1.0111	0.90136975	10 000 000	9 113 850
3 years	1.0111	0.85354513	10 000 000	8 630 290
			Total	27 440 842

*This is considered a leap year.

Table 21.5

Date	Zero rate (365)	Implicit rate (360)	European cap strike 5.5%	
			European value	Cash value (€)
Today			18.00%	(volatility)
1 year	5.104	5.46	0.358	36 201
2 years	5.322	5.54	0.522	52 762
3 years	5.420	5.65	0.652	65 884
			Total	154 847

Cap value = €154 847
Nominal = 1.55%

In our example it will be

$$\text{Spread} = \frac{59\,359}{27\,440\,842} = 0.22\%$$

In short, it can be seen that at equilibrium the buyer obtains a smaller cost than an alternative standard cap. Table 21.5 shows the figures for a 3 year European cap with strike at 5.50%.

In spread terms, this cap would be worth +0.57%. Put another way, the person buying the step-up triggered cap assumes a financing cost at Euribor + 0.22% with ceiling at 5.50% or 7.50%. But if there were a hedge with a maximum ceiling at 5.50%, then the financing cost would be Euribor + 0.57%.

Valuation

Valuation of the step-up triggered cap is reduced to calculating the value of the two barrier caps which the buyer receives. In any case, it is extremely simple. Here are the relevant caps:

- Up-and-out cap with $K_0 = x$ with barrier $H = y$ is equivalent to a position on

$$\text{European cap with } K_1 = K_0 = x$$
$$- \text{ European cap with } K_2 = H = y$$
$$- \text{ digital cap with } K_3 = H \qquad (21.2)$$
$$(\text{payoff} = H - K_0 = y - x)$$

- Up-and-in cap with $K_0 = y$ with barrier $H = y$ is equivalent to a position on

$$\text{European cap with } K_1 = H = y \qquad (21.3)$$

where

x = lower limit or ceiling
y = higher limit or ceiling
K = strike
H = barrier

The standard caps would be evaluated by Black 76 in equation (14.1). The model for the digital cap is equation (16.1)

From the holder's viewpoint (the holder has rising interest rate cover), the structure's value will be given by

$$\text{Price} = \text{knockout cap}[\text{underlying}(r_{\text{imp}_i}), \text{strike}(r_{\text{fixed}}),$$
$$\text{barrier}, \text{time}_i, r_i, \text{volatility}]$$
$$+ \text{knock-in cap}[\text{underlying}(r_{\text{imp}_i}), \text{strike}(r_{\text{fixed}}),$$
$$\text{barrier}, \text{time}_i, r_i, \text{volatility}]$$

where

r = risk-free interest rate
r_{imp} = implicit or forward interest rate

The price may be expressed as an interest rate spread throughout the structure, or as the present value in the relevant currency.

22

CONSTANT MATURITY BOND

Definition and commercial presentation

Constant maturity bonds are assets or notes with floating rate periodic coupons linked to long-term interest rates. The frequency in which those interests are paid usually differs from the term of the interest rate index to which they are linked. Their structure is intimately linked to constant maturity swaps (CMS), whose main feature is the swap in floating interest by both branches. One pays interest linked to any floating money market rate, and the other pays interest linked to the long-term interest rates of financial instruments.

The big difference in relation to a standard floating rate note (FRN) lies in the risk assumed. In a standard FRN (Chapter 13) it is only attributable to the coupon already fixed, whereas in a CMT there is risk in the interest rate, specifically the curve, for all future cash flows.

Various names are used for instruments which have essentially the same structure. Here are some of them. The constant maturity treasury (CMT) is a floating rate bond issued by sovereign governments. Instead of being index-linked to short-term rates, it is linked to the yield to maturity (YTM) with its own benchmarks of fixed terms, or failing that, it is linked to IRS rates. Spain has TIC (tipo de interés constante); France has TEC (taux d'échéance constante) and Germany has REX; these are floating rate bonds from private or semi-official issuers. Their periodic interest index is linked to the long-term bond yields, or to IRS rates. All these instruments have the same structure; the only difference is in the curves for discounting the flows and calculating the forward interest rates.

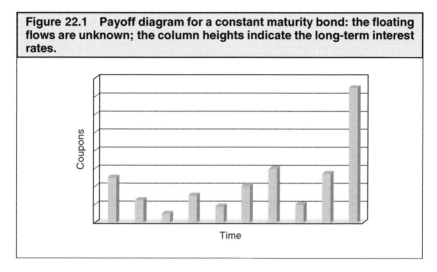

Figure 22.1   Payoff diagram for a constant maturity bond: the floating flows are unknown; the column heights indicate the long-term interest rates.

Maturity is usually medium and long term, from 10 to 20 years; they are generally issued at par, and they guarantee the principal and offer a percentage of the reference index as coupon payments.

$$\text{Payoff} = \text{coupons(long-term rates index)} + \text{principal}$$

Figure 22.1 shows the payoff diagram.

Risks

There is a risk in interest rates for all future flows. It exists in all movements of the interest rate curve between the short term, marking the frequency of interest payments, and the long term, acting as reference at the time they are fixed. Besides that, considering that these structures have a special convexity component in their cash flows, a new kind of risk is generated. So it is affected, in some way, by the expected volatility of the underlying, also called implied volatility. This will be examined in the section on valuation.

Let's look at the distinguishing risk factors in a constant maturity bond structure (CMB) and compare them with a standard FRN. In a standard FRN the interest rate risk is in the coupon that is already fixed, since for the residue there is no risk once the reference index has corresponded with the accrual periods and interest payments. In a CMB the frequency of interest payments does not correspond with the index term that is the reference for fixing the interest. In the simplest case of a CMB which pays annual interest linked to a 10 year IRS rate, whoever acquires the title then runs the risk of 10 year rates falling (collecting lower coupons) while the short-term rates stay stable or may even rise. This would increase the downside, where an increase in financing cost might theoretically occur in the title. Put another way, rises in short-term rates, which are the natural investment alternative when there are falls in long-term rates (those linked to the CMB), would generate a relatively major loss in the investment.

Construction

The issuer of the CMB is issuing a floating rate bond (convertible at fixed rate through a standard IRS) and selling a constant maturity swap, on which he receives the long-term floating rate, in exchange for payment of the short-term floating rate (Libor, Euribor, etc.). Payment of short-term rates will be financed with the principal obtained, and invested in deposits with the same term as the frequency of the swap Libor/Euribor branch (e.g. 6 month standard type). Here is a summary of the operations:

- Sell a CMS. The issuer pays the short-term rate and receives the long-term rate. These flows must have the same frequency as agreed on the bond offered to the investors.
- Pay the investor of the bond issue the agreed long-term percentage rate, obtained from the previous CMS swap.
- With the principal received, invest short-term (at the same rate as operated in one of the CMS branches) and pay this amount to the CMS swap counterparty.

Example

There is a 3 year CMT on which the issuer makes annual payments in euros equal to 74.50% of the 10 year IRS rate. Let's assume the CMT is issued at par through a unit nominal of €10 million, and let's assume the coupon is fixed and paid in each of the three years on an appointed date. The fixing will take as reference the IRS rate published on the stipulated date by any agreed financial information vendor.

Indicative terms

Description	Bond in euros with variable coupons linked to a 10 year IRS rate, payable annually
Nominal	€10 000 000
Issue price	100%
Interest	74.50% of the 10 year IRS rate
Term	3 years
Amortisation	€59 359 or 0.22% at 3 year annual spread in three payments

The structure consists of the floating rate bond issue, which is 'swapped' with any financial institution using a CMS, through which the issuer will receive annually the 10 year IRS at the percentage quoted on the market (at equilibrium it is assumed the investor will be offered 74.5% in this example). In exchange, on the CMS the issuer will have to pay the agreed money market index (let's assume 6 month Euribor payable six-monthly). With the principal received, i.e. €10 million, the issuer invests for the 6 months and renews on each maturity date, in order to pay this amount to the CMS counterparty. In this way, once he has collected from the previous CMS, the issuer can pay the investor of the bond issue the 74.5% rate determined by the 10 year IRS.

The 74.5% in this example results from the present value, at market conditions, in the floating flows estimated for 6 months (the FRA rates or forward), which only represent 74.5% of the present value in those corresponding to the 10 IRS forward rates estimated for the next three years.

Table 22.1

SIX-MONTHLY STANDARD FLOATING BRANCH

Years	Discount factor	Fixed rate (%)	Flow (€)	Current value (€)
0.50	0.98270	3.50	176.944	173.883
1.00	0.96202	4.21	214.983	206.817
1.50	0.03878	4.92	247.537	232.382
2.00	0.91567	4.94	252.315	231.038
2.50	0.89113	5.48	275.357	245.300
3.00	0.86681	5.49	280.611	243.237
			Total	1332.738

ANNUAL LONG-TERM FLOATING BRANCH

Years	Discount factor	Fixed IRS (%)	Convexity adjustment (%)	Flow (€)	Current value (€)
1.00	0.96202	6.24	0.0345	637.623	613.403
2.00	0.91567	6.45	0.0599	650.922	596.032
3.00	0.86681	6.61	0.0793	668.863	579.778
4.00	0.81790				
5.00	0.77057				
6.00	0.72411				
7.00	0.67852				
8.00	0.63403				
9.00	0.59338				
10.00	0.55563				
11.00	0.52056				
12.00	0.48686				
13.00	0.45460				
				Total	1789.213

Given the interest rate curve in Table 22.1 (with its corresponding discount factors), let's take a look at the pricing displayed in this example.

As may be observed, €1 332 738 represents 74.50% of €1 789 213, through which this CMS would be quoted at that percentage. If that is so, the issuer of the CMT bond would sell this CMS to a financial institution (receiving long-term and paying short-term). Each time the issuer collects the 10 year rate through the financial institution's CMS (three times during the three years), he will be able to pay the investors the agreed coupon, assuming in the last instance the 6 month floating cost. 'Extraordinary' profits might be obtained by the issuer if, instead of agreeing on the issue to pay 74.5%, he will pay perhaps 72%, which is below the previous conditions and market curve. In this case the issue price would not be suitable for the investor if it came out at par. For the investor, who receives an offer to collect 72% of the 10 year IRS rate, the breakeven price would be 97.5%, i.e. 2.5% lower; this is to compensate for the smaller participation offered on the reference index.

Valuation

Valuation of a CMB is simple once we know the underlying CMS value in the structure. In fact, it can be performed in three steps.

Step 1

Calculate the present values in the standard floating branch of a CMS and in the floating branch linked to the long-term rate. In its last branch, the CMS must have the same interest payment frequency in the coupons offered on the CMT, and the same maturity. The value of the CMS is given by the difference in the present values of the two branches:

$$\text{CMS value} = \sum_{i=1}^{n} (r_f)_i \times \text{nominal} \times \text{YF}_i \times \text{DF}_i$$

$$- \sum_{i=1}^{n} (\text{FS}_i + \text{CA}_i) \times \text{nominal} \times \text{YF}_i \times \text{DF}_i \qquad (22.1)$$

where

r_f = forward interest rate

FS = forward swap = $(\text{DF}_0 - \text{DF}_n) \Big/ \sum_{i=1}^{n} \text{YF}_i \, \text{DF}_i$

CA = convexity adjustment

Use the appropriate CA for this type of flow. Where the flows are fixed and paid on the same date, then the adjustment proposed by Brotherton-Ratcliffe and Iben is valid. Here are its fundamental parameters:

- Forward swap rate FS_i
- Zero coupon rates r_i on relevant dates (maturity dates of the flows)
- Time T in years until the flow matures
- Volatility σ of the forward swap

The volatility may be obtained from the swaptions market, in terms of implied volatility levels. The model is as follows:

$$CA_i = 0.5(FS)^2\sigma^2 T \frac{P''(FS)}{P'(FS)} \tag{22.2}$$

$$P'(FS) = \frac{(1 + FS)T_n}{(1 + FS)^{1+T_n}} + \sum_{i=1}^{n-1} \frac{FS \times T_i}{(1 + FS)^{1+T_i}} \tag{22.3}$$

$$P''(FS) = \frac{(1 + FS)T_n(1 + T_n)}{(1 + FS)^{2+T_n}} + \sum_{i=1}^{n-1} \frac{FS(1 + T_i)T_i}{(1 + FS)^{2+T_i}} \tag{22.4}$$

An adjustment is required if the date of fixing the flow and its payment do not coincide, namely, when the difference between the dates does not coincide with the term of the reference index. Hull (2000, p. 554) proposes a good approximation for the adjustment as an alternative to using numerical integration methods such as Romberg or Simpson (Gerald and Wheatley 1999, pp. 377–85). It requires the correlation coefficient between the reference rate and the rate during the period between fixing and payment, and it is given by the following equation:

$$CA_i = 0.5(FS)^2\sigma^2 T \frac{P''(FS)}{P'(FS)} - \frac{FS \times \delta r \sigma_{FS}\sigma_r \rho T}{1 + r\delta} \tag{22.5}$$

where

r = implicit or forward deposit rate between fixing and payment
δ = period of time in years between fixing and payment
ρ = correlation coefficient between reference rate and the rate during the period between fixing and payment
σ_{FS} = implied volatility of the forward swap (swaption)
σ_r = implied volatility of the implicit FRA (cap)
T = time in years until flow matures

Step 2

Having found the present values in the two branches, the value which represents the standard variable branch, with respect to the branch linked to the long-term rate, will be the percentage of the long-term rate that must be offered by the issuer in conditions of equilibrium. In our example the CMS quoted a rate of 74.5%. Therefore, at equilibrium, the issuer who was selling to a bank to hedge the issue, could offer annual coupons at 74.5%. This is the rate determined by the 10 year IRS, each year on the preset date.

Step 3

The revaluation of a CMB already issued on the market will be equal to the difference between the CMS value at the outset and the CMS value at time *t*. Moreover, this takes into consideration the cash flows already realised since the title was acquired, and turned into capital at the rate that existed between payment of the flow and the actual moment. As with a CMB that has already been issued, participation in the reference index to determine the coupon has already been determined at the moment of issue, and its revaluation will require calculating the breakeven price for the new conditions. So the structure's value will be given by

Price = present value of the principal

+ (CMS value at issue − current CMS value)

APPENDIX A

TEN GOLDEN RULES

Quality considerations are just as important as technical competence. The most relevant aspect for the investor is to be able to separate the structure into its component parts. By evaluating its components, he will get to know the market price of these products. This is the most difficult task. The 'retail' investor must assume that, on certain occasions, the total value of a structured product may not be exactly equal to the theoretical sum of its parts. Perhaps this appears to contradict some of our earlier ideas. But that is not so. Keep in mind the cost reductions in the process of structuring. These cost reductions are smaller in the 'retail' field, so the costs may be correspondingly greater.

In structured products where options may be involved, the structure will not always be outlined in the purchase of the basic asset and purchase of one or other options by the investor. In many structured products the investor sells options. In this sense, remember that the seller is selling volatility with their associated complications in management and/or hedging. 'Selling volatility' means taking positions that will only obtain profits in situations where the price is stable in the structure's reference instrument.

Some more general thoughts may be conveniently summarised as a set of ten golden rules:

1. Investors should not look for a structured product if it really isn't necessary.
2. It is difficult for an individual investor to get the same advantages as a group of investors; cost reductions are usually greater for a wholesale structure than for a retail structure.
3. All that glitters is not gold.
4. Never swap a pound for a penny without raising a charge.

5. A structured product should not be purchased and then immediately hedged.
6. Hedging of structured products could make sense when taking earned profits or making stop-losses.
7. Even complex structures started out quite simple.
8. Simplicity is the investor's best friend.
9. Complexity is the structurer's best friend.
10. Whenever you hedge, make sure you're on firm ground. Depending on your business objective, either cover any risk from the outset, or leave it at risk till the end. Patches never work well.

APPENDIX B

CHARACTERISTICS FROM THE BUYER'S VIEWPOINT

Structure	Involved with	Expectations for underlying	Expectations for volatility	Investment/ financing	Derivative product	Profitability	Principal
EQUITY STRUCTURES							
Warrants	equity	bullish	bullish	investment	buy	variable	NG (premium)
Equity deposit	equity	bullish	bullish	investment	buy	variable	G/NG
Asian deposit	equity	bullish	bullish	investment	buy	variable	G/NG
Straddle with knockout	equity	mixed	mixed	investment	buy	variable	G
Digital range	equity	stable	bearish	investment	sell	variable	G
Reverse convertible	equity	bullish	bearish	investment	sell	variable	G/NG
Ladder bond	equity	bullish	bullish	investment	buy	variable	G/NG
Basket bond	equity	bullish	bullish	investment	buy	variable	G/NG
Spread bond	equity	bullish	bullish	investment	buy	variable	G/NG
Best-of bond	equity	bullish	bullish	investment	buy	variable	G/NG
FIXED INCOME STRUCTURES							
Floating rate note (FRN)	interest rates	bullish	nil	investment	buy	variable	G
Reverse FRN	interest rates	bearish	nil	investment	buy	variable (A)	G
Collared FRN	interest rates	bullish	nil/bullish	investment	buy/sell	variable (A)	G
Digital range	interest rates	stable	bearish	investment	sell	variable	G
Step-up callable	interest rates	mixed	bearish	investment	sell	fixed/rise	G
Reset note	interest rates	bullish	nil/bearish	investment	sell	variable	G
Participating swap	interest rates	mixed	bullish	financing	buy	variable	NE
Performance swap	interest rates	mixed	bearish	financing	sell	variable	NE
Step-up triggered cap	interest rates	bullish	bullish	financing	buy	variable	NE
Constant maturity bond	interest rates	bullish (L)	bullish (M)	investment	buy	variable	G

G = guaranteed, NG = not guaranteed, G/NG = can be structured in both forms, L = long-term rates, M = moderately, A = limited, NE = no swap of principal exists.

BIBLIOGRAPHY

Ahn, H.-D., Figlewski, S. and Gao, B. (1999) Pricing discrete barrier options with an adaptive mesh model. *Journal of Derivatives*, vol. 6, no. 4.

Andersen, L. and Brotherton-Ratcliffe, R. (1996) Exact exotics. *Risk*, October.

Barclays (1995) Asian/average price options. April.

Baxter, M. and Rennie, A. (1996) *Financial calculus: an introduction to derivative pricing.* Cambridge: Cambridge University Press.

Bessis, J. (1998) *Risk management in banking.* New York: John Wiley & Sons.

Bierwag, G. O. (1991) *Análisis de la duración: la gestión del riesgo de tipo de interés.* Madrid: Alianza.

Bowie, J. and Carr, P. (1994) Static simplicity. *Risk*, August.

Boyle, P. and Lau, S. H. (1994) Bumping up against the barrier with the binomial method. *Journal of Derivatives*, vol. 1, no. 4.

Butler, C. (1999) *Mastering value at risk: a step-by-step guide to understanding and applying VaR.* London: Financial Times/Prentice Hall.

Campbell, J. Y. *et al.* (1997) *The econometrics of financial markets.* New York: Princeton University Press.

Carr, P. and Chou, A. (1997) Breaking barriers. *Risk*, September.

Chesney, M. *et al.* (1997) Parisian pricing. *Risk*, January.

Cheuk, T. and Vorst, T. (1996) *Breaking down barriers. Risk*, April.

_____ (1996) Complex barrier options. *Journal of Derivatives*, vol. 4, no. 1.

Cheung, W. and Lam, W. (1996) Thai'd and tested. *Asia Risk*, July.

Chew, L. (1996) *Managing derivative risks: the use and abuse of leverage.* New York: John Wiley & Sons.

Chorafas, D. N. (1997) *Market risk amendment.* New York: McGraw-Hill.

Chriss, N. (1997) *Black–Scholes and beyond: option pricing models.* Chicago: Irwin.

Chriss, N. and Ong, M. (1995) Digital defused. *Risk*, December.

Clewlow, L. and Strickland, C. (1998) *Implementing derivatives models.* New York: John Wiley & Sons.

Cornyn, A. G., Lederman, J. and Klein, R. A. (1997) *Controlling and managing interest-rate risk.* Englewood Cliffs NJ: Prentice Hall

Das, S. (ed.) (1998) *Risk management and financial derivatives: a guide to the mathematics.* New York: McGraw-Hill.

Deacon, M. (1996) Short solution. *Asia Risk*, April.

Dewynne, J. and Wilmott, P. (1993) Partial to the exotic. *Risk*, March.

Douglas, L. G. (1990) *Bond risk analysis: a guide to duration and convexity*. New York: New York Institute of Finance.

Dupire, B. (1993) Model art. *Risk*, September.

_____ (1994) Pricing with a smile. *Risk*, January

Fabozzi, F. J. (1999) *Duration, convexity, and other bond risk measures*. New Hope: Frank J. Fabozzi Associates.

Falloon, W. (1995) Hedges for export. *Risk*, July.

Francis, J. C. (ed.) *et al.* (2000) *The handbook of equity derivatives*. New York: John Wiley & Sons.

Frishling, F. (1997) Barrier rife. *Australian and New Zealand Risk*, August.

Gastineau, G. (1993) An introduction to special-purpose derivatives: options with a payout depending on more than one variable. *Journal of Derivatives*, vol. 1, no. 1.

_____ (1994) An introduction to special-purpose derivatives: rate differential swaps and deferred strike options. *Journal of Derivatives*, vol. 1, no. 3.

_____ (1994) An introduction to special-purpose derivatives: roll-up puts, roll-down calls, and contingent premium options. *Journal of Derivatives*, vol. 1, no. 4.

Geman, H. and Eydeland, A. (1995) Domino effect. *Risk*, April.

Gentle, J. E. (1998) *Random number generation and Monte Carlo methods*. New York: Springer.

Gerald, C. and Wheatley, P. (1999) *Applied numerical analysis*, 6th edn. Reading MA: Addison Wesley Longman.

Gray, G. and Watson, J. (eds) (1994) *Swaps compendium*. London: Euromoney.

Hart, I. and Ross, M. (1994) Striking continuity. *Risk*, June.

Heynen, R. and Kat, H. (1994) Crossing barriers. *Risk*, June.

_____ (1994) Selective memory. *Risk*, November.

_____ (1996) Brick by brick. *Risk*, June.

Hsu, H. (1997) Surprised parties. *Risk*, April.

Hull, J. C. (2000) *Options, futures and other derivatives*. Englewood Cliffs NJ: Prentice Hall.

Hull, J. C. and White, A. (1993) Efficient procedures for valuing path dependent options. *Journal of Derivatives*, vol. 1, no. 1.

Hunt, P. J. and Kennedy, J. E. (2000) *Financial derivatives in theory and practice*. New York: John Wiley & Sons.

Jorion, P. (1995) *Value at risk: the new benchmark for controlling market risk*. Chicago: Irwin.

Judd, K. M. (1999) *Numerical methods in economics*. Cambridge: MIT Press.

Kat, H. (1994) Contingent premium options. *Journal of Derivatives*, vol. 1, no. 4.

Kat, H. and Verdonk, L. (1995) Tree surgery. *Risk*, February.

Levy, E. and Mantion, F. (1997) Approximate valuation of discrete lookback and barrier options. *Net exposure*, November.

_____ (1997) Discrete by nature. *Risk*, January.

Linetsky, V. (1998) Structuring, pricing and hedging complex barrier options. *Asian Risk*, January.

_____ (1998) Steps to the barrier, *Risk*, April.

Liu, R. Y. (1995) The alchemy of Asian exotics. *Asia Risk*, November.

Lyden, S. (1996) Reference check: a bibliography of exotic options models. *Journal of Derivatives*, vol. 4, no. 1.

Mikosch, T. (1998) *Elementary stochastic calculus with finance in view*. New York: World Scientific.

Murphy, D. (1997) Setting the scene. *Risk*, June.

Musiela, M. and Rutkowski, M. (1998) *Martingale methods in financial modelling*. New York: Springer.

Natwest (1995) Opciones exóticas. August.

Paribas (1994) Equity hedging call with rebate. April.

_____ (1994) Foreign exchange hedging contingent option. April.

Pearson, N. D. (1995) An efficient approach for pricing spread options. *Journal of Derivatives*, vol. 3, no. 1.

Pechtl, A. (1995) Classified information. *Risk*, June.

Peng, S. Y. and Dattatreya, R. E. (1995) *The structured note market: the definitive guide for investors, traders and issuers*. Chicago: Probus.

Phoa, W. (1998) *Advanced fixed income analytics*. New Hope: Frank J. Fabozzi Associates.

Piskunov, N. (1978) *Cálculo differential e integral*. Barcelona: Montaner y Simón.

Ramanlal, P. (1997) Which warrant? *Risk*, January.

Rebonato, R. (1997) *Interest-rate options models: understanding, analysing and using models for exotic interest-rate options*. Chichester: John Wiley & Sons.

_____ (1999) *Volatility and correlation in the pricing of equity, FX, and interest-rate options*. New York: John Wiley & Sons.

Reed, N. (1995) Tales of exotica. *Risk*, June.

Richtken, P. (1995) On pricing barrier options. *Journal of Derivatives*, vol. 3, no. 2.

Rubinstein, M. and Reiner, E. (1991) Unscrambling the binary code. *Risk*, October.

Sánchez, F. and Tarriba, J. (1999) Documento monográfico de riesgos. BSCH, October.

Smithson, C. (1997) Path-dependency. *Risk*, April.

Smithson, C. and Cham, W. (1997) Multifactor options. *Risk*, May.

Stetson, C., Marshall, S. and Loebell, D. (1995) Laudable lattices. *Risk*, December.

Stetson, C., Stokke, S. and Spinner, A. (1997) Markov esteem. *Risk*, January.

Taleb, N. (1990) *Dynamic hedging: managing vanilla and exotic options*. New York: John Wiley & Sons.

Tavella, D. and Randall, C. (2000) *Pricing financial instruments: the finite difference method*. New York: John Wiley & Sons.

Tompkins, R. G. (1994) *Options explained*. Basingstoke: Macmillan.

_____ (1997) Static vs. dynamic hedging of exotic options. *Net Exposure*, November.

Trippi, R. R. and Chance, D. M. (1993) Quick valuation of the Bermuda capped option. *Journal of Portfolio Management*, vol. 20, no. 1.

Turnbull, S. (1992) The price is right. *Risk*, April.

Vidal, J. (2000) Documento monográfico de riesgos. BSCH, September.

Vose, D. (1996) *Quantitative risk analysis: a guide to Monte Carlo simulation modelling*. New York: John Wiley & Sons.

Wei, J. Z. (1998) Valuation of discrete barrier options by interpolations. *Journal of Derivatives*, vol. 6, no. 1.

Wilmott, P. (1995) *Mathematics of financial derivatives: a student introduction*. Cambridge: Cambridge University Press.

_____ (1998) *Derivatives: the theory and practice of financial engineering*. Chichester: John Wiley & Sons.

Yu, G. G. (1994) Financial instruments to lock in payoffs. *Journal of Derivatives*, vol. 1, no. 3.

Zhang, P. G. (1995) Flexible arithmetic Asian options. *Journal of Derivatives*, vol. 2, no. 3.

_____ (1998) *Exotic options: a guide to second generation options*. Singapore: World Scientific.

Zvan, R. *et al.* (1998) Swing low. Swing high. *Risk*, March.

INDEX

absolute sensitivity (SA)   18
accrual notes   63
American options   19–20, 133
American warrants   34
amortisation   133, 138
appendices   179–82
Asian deposits   47–54, 48, 182
Asian warrants   34
assets   3
   see also underlying assets
   equity   63–9
   fixed income   17–19
   options   20–1, 43
availability   45, 53

barrier options
   performance swaps   154, 158
   step-up triggered caps   164
   straddle with knockout deposit
      57–61
basket bonds   83–90, 84–5, 182
Bermudan options   133
Bermudan warrants   34
best-of bonds   99–105, 100, 182
best-of call options   101
Black–Scholes model   20
bootstrapping   16
built-in surcharges   65

call options
   Asian deposits   49, 51
   best-of   101
   equity deposits   43
   percentage best-of   103

share basket   86
spread bonds   95
straddle with knockout deposit   59,
   61
underlying assets   43, 49
up-and-out   59, 61
calls
   basic concepts   19–22
   bonds   88, 95, 103
   deposits   73
   digital ranges   65–6, 129
   European   20, 44–5, 88
   knockout   78–9, 78
   rho   22
   swaptions   135, 137
   theta   21
   warrants   33
capitalisation   13
caps
   collared floating rate notes   124–5
   knockout   162, 163–4, 164, 166, 167
   performance swaps   155–8, 157
   reverse floating rate notes   119–20
   step-up triggered   161–70, 162–4,
      166–8
cash flow assessments   13
cash operations   13–15
CMB *see* constant maturity bonds
CMS *see* constant maturity swaps
CMT *see* constant maturity treasury
collared floating rate notes   121–5, 122,
   182
constant maturity bonds (CMB)
   171–7, 172, 174, 182
constant maturity swaps (CMS)   171,
   173–5

constant maturity treasury (CMT)   10,
    171, 173
construction
    Asian deposits   49–51
    basket bonds   86–8
    best-of bonds   101–3
    collared floating rate notes   122–4
    constant maturity bonds   173–5, *174*
    digital ranges   65–7, 129–31
    equity deposits   43–4
    floating rate notes   110–13
    ladder bonds   79–81
    participating swaps   149–51, *150–1*
    performance swaps   154–7, *157*
    reset notes   140–4, *141–2*
    reverse convertibles   73–5
    reverse floating rate notes   116–19
    spread bonds   93–5
    step-up callable bonds   135–7
    step-up triggered caps   164–9, *166–8*
    straddle with knockout deposit   57–9
    warrants   36–7
corridor notes   63, 65
    interest rates   127–32, *128*
covering purchased structures   10–11
currency convention   13

D *see* Macaulay duration
delta   21, 69
deposits
    Asian   47–54, *48*, 182
    calls   73
    equity   41–5, *42*, 182
    ladder bonds   79
    risk-free zero coupons   12
    straddle with knockout deposit   57
    zero coupons   112
digital calls   65–6, 129
digital puts   65–6, 129
digital ranges   182
    equity assets   63–9, *64*
    interest rates   127–32, *128*
discount factors   13–17
dividend payments   20–1
down-and-out put options (DO)   59, 61
duration (price elasticity)   18–16

equity
    assets   63–9

deposits   41–5, *42*, 182
    structures   31–106, 182
European calls   20, 44–5, 88
European options
    basic concepts   19–20
    basket bonds   88
    equity deposits   44–5
    reverse convertibles   75
    step-up callable bonds   133
European warrants   33–9, *34*

financial options, basic concepts   19–22
fixed income
    assets   17–19
    structures   107–78, 182
fixed interest rate instalments   13
fixed rate bonds   110, 116
floating rate notes (FRN)   10, 109–14,
    110, 112–14
    characteristics   182
    constant maturity bonds   171–3
floors   149–52
FRN *see* floating rate notes

gains   26
gamma   21
Gerald, C.   103
golden rules   179–80
guaranteed products   11–12

hamster   63
historical value at risk methods   23,
    25–9
Hull, J. C.   52, 119

implied volatility   21, 69
in the money (ITM)   68
index movements   122
instrument valuation   13–29
interbank deposit interest rates   13
interbank deposit rate discount factors
    15
interbank market rates   16
interest payment frequencies   16
interest rate curves   11
    constant maturity bonds   *174, 175*
    step-up triggered caps   166–8, *166,
    168*

interest rate swaps (IRS)   15–17
  collared floating rate notes   122
  constant maturity bonds   171
  floating rate notes   110
  participating swaps   149
  reverse floating rate notes   117–19,
    119
  step-up callable bonds   135
interest rates   13–17, 127–32, 128
  see also fixed interest...
investment conditions   9–10
investor risks   10
  Asian deposits   48–9
  basket bonds   84
  best-of bonds   100–1, 100
  digital ranges   64–5, 128
  equity deposits   42
  ladder bonds   79
  reverse convertibles   72–3
  spread bonds   93
  step-up triggered caps   161–3, 162–4
  straddle with knockout deposit   56
IRS see interest rate swaps
issuer risks   10
  Asian deposits   49
  basket bonds   84–6
  best-of bonds   100–1
  digital ranges   65, 128
  equity deposits   42
  ladder bonds   79
  reverse convertibles   73
  spread bonds   93
  step-up triggered caps   164
  straddle with knockout deposit   56–7
ITM see in the money

knock-in caps   162–4, 166, 168
  performance swaps   155–8, 157
knockout
  barriers   57, 59–61
  calls   78–9, 78
  caps   162, 163–4, 164, 166, 167

ladder bonds   77–82, 78, 182
ladder options   79, 81–2
liabilities   3–4
losses   26

Macaulay duration (D)   19

maturity
  Asian deposits   47, 51
  basket bonds   83, 88
  best-of bonds   99, 103
  bonds   171–7, 172, 174
  collared floating rate notes   121
  constant maturity bonds   171, 172,
    182
  digital ranges   63–4, 127
  equity deposits   41, 44–5
  floating rate notes   109
  ladder bonds   77, 81
  participating swaps   147
  performance swaps   153
  reset notes   139
  reverse convertibles   71, 75
  reverse floating rate notes   115
  spread bonds   91, 95
  step-up callable bonds   133
  step-up triggered caps   161
  straddle with knockout deposit   55,
    59
MD see modified duration
models, Black–Scholes   20
modified duration (MD)   18
Monte Carlo methods   23
Morgan, J. P.   23, 25

net present value (NPV)   21
non-guaranteed products   12
NPV see net present value

options
  see also call options; European options
  American   19–20, 133
  asset   20–1, 43
  basic concepts   19–22
  Bermudan   133
  best-of call   101
  down-and-out puts   59, 61
  financial   19–22
  ladder   79, 81–2
  percentage best-of call options   103
  step-up callable bonds   133
  values   44–5, 53

parametric value at risk   23–9
parity   36
part-time knock-in caps   155–8, 157

participating swaps   147–52, *148*,
    150–1, 182
payoff
    Asian deposits   47, *48*
    basket bonds   83, *84*
    best-of bonds   99, *100*
    collared floating rate notes   121, *122*
    constant maturity bonds   172, *172*
    digital ranges   63–4, *64*, 65, 68, 127,
        128
    equity deposits   41, *42*
    floating rate notes   109, *110*
    ladder bonds   77, *78*
    participating swaps   147–8, *148*
    performance swaps   153, *154*
    reset notes   139, *140*
    reverse convertibles   71, *72*
    reverse floating rate notes   115, *116*
    spread bonds   91, *92*
    step-up callable bonds   133–4, *134*
    step-up triggered caps   161, *162*
    straddle with knockout deposit   55,
        56
    warrants   *34*, 35
Pearson, N. D.   97
percentage best-of call options   103
percentiles (losses/gains)   26
performance swaps   153–9, *154*, *157–8*,
    182
periodic coupon bonds   17–18
price generation   26
proprietary values   26
purchased floating rate notes   116
purchased structures   10–11
puts
    basic concepts   19–22
    digital ranges   65–6, 129
    rho   22
    straddle with knockout deposit   59,
        61
    theta   22
    warrants   33

rebates   63
reference share call spread   93
reference stock price index (SPI)   43, 63
reset notes   139–45, *140–2*, 182
reverse convertibles   12, 71–6, *72*, 182
reverse floating rate notes   115–20,
    116, *119*, 182

rho   22
risk-free zero coupon deposits   12
RiskMetrics   23, 25
risks
    see also value at risk
    Asian deposits   47–9
    basket bonds   84–6, *85*
    best-of bonds   100–1, *100*
    collared floating rate notes   121–2
    constant maturity bonds   172–3
    digital ranges   64–5, 128
    equity deposits   42
    floating rate notes   109–10
    introduction   4
    ladder bonds   77–9
    measurements   10, 13–29
    participating swaps   148–9
    performance swaps   154
    reset notes   139–40
    reverse convertibles   72–3
    reverse floating rate notes   115–16
    spread bonds   91–3, *92*
    step-up callable bonds   134–5
    step-up triggered caps   161–4, *162–4*
    straddle with knockout deposit   56–7
    warrants   35–6, *35*

SA *see* absolute sensitivity
sensitivity   18, 35–6, *35*
share basket call options   86
share-bearing warrants   35–6, *35*
simulation methods   25–9
solid fixed rate bonds   116
SPI *see* reference stock price index
spot barriers   57–8
spot operations   13–15
spread bonds   91–8, *92*, 182
spread call options, spread bonds   95
step-up callable bonds   133–8, 182
step-up triggered caps   161–70, *162–4*,
    166–8, 182
stock price index *see* reference stock...
straddle with knockout deposit   55–61,
    56, 182
strike prices   33
structuring schemes   11–12
swaptions   135, 137, 140–4

temporary series calculations   25
theta   21–2

underlying assets
  call options   43, 49
  price sensitivity   21
  price variations   21, 69
UO *see* up-and-out call options
up-and-in caps   158–9
up-and-out call options (UO)   59, 61
up-and-out caps   169

valuations   13–29
  Asian deposits   51–4
  basket bonds   88–90
  best-of bonds   103–5
  Black–Scholes model   20
  collared floating rate notes   124–5
  constant maturity bonds   175–7
  digital ranges   67–9, 131–2
  equity deposits   44–5
  floating rate notes   113–14
  ladder bonds   81–2
  participating swaps   151–2, *151*
  performance swaps   157–9, *158*
  reset notes   144–5
  reverse convertibles   75–6
  reverse floating rate notes   119–20
  spread bonds   95–8
  step-up callable bonds   137–8
  step-up triggered caps   169–70
  straddle with knockout deposit
    59–61

warrants   37–9, *37*
value at risk (VaR)   22–9
variable income asset warrants   35
vector of sensitivities   25
vega   21, 69
Vidal, J.   96, 97
volatility
  basket bonds   84–6, *85*, 87
  best-of bonds   100–1, *100*
  constant maturity bonds   176
  digital ranges   69
  implied   21
  spread bonds   91–3, *92*

warrants   33–9, *34–5, 37*, 182
Wheatley, P.   103

yield to maturity (YTM)   18–19, 171

zero coupon deposits   11–12
zero rate bonds   93, 101
zero rate deposits
  Asian deposits   49, 51
  equity deposits   43
  ladder bonds   79
  straddle with knockout deposit   57
zero rate liabilities   86
Zhang, P. G.   96

Printed in Poland
by Amazon Fulfillment
Poland Sp. z o.o., Wrocław
16 October 2020